Columbus
DICTIONARY

Columbus
DICTIONARY

by

Foster Provost
Duquesne University

Omnigraphics, Inc.

Penobscot Building • Detroit, MI 48226

Library of Congress Cataloging-in-Publication Data

Provost, Foster.
    Columbus dictionary / by Foster Provost.
      p. cm.
    Includes bibliographical references.
    ISBN 1-55888-158-1 (acid-free paper)
    1. Columbus, Christopher—Dictionaries, indexes, etc. 2. America-
-Discovery and exploration—Spanish—Dictionaries. I. Title.
E111.P96 1991
970.01'5'03—dc20
                                        91-29120
                                             CIP

Foster Provost, Editor

Omnigraphics, Inc.

Laurie Lanzen Harris, Vice President, Editorial Director
Frank R. Abate, Vice President, Dictionaries
Annie M. Brewer, Vice President, Research
Peter E. Ruffner, Vice President, Administration
James A. Sellgren, Vice President, Operations and Finance
Eric F. Berger, Production Manager

***

Fredrick G. Ruffner, Jr., Publisher

Omnigraphics, Inc.

ISBN 1-55888-158-1

The information in this publication was compiled from the sources cited and from other sources considered reliable. While every possible effort has been made to ensure reliability, the publisher will not assume liability for damages caused by inaccuracies in the data, and makes no warranty, express or implied, on the accuracy of the information contained herein.

∞
This book is printed on acid-free paper meeting the ANSI Z39.48 Standard. The infinity symbol that appears above indicates that the paper in this book meets that standard.

Printed in the United States of America

Contents

Preface   vii

Introduction   ix

Bibliography   xi

A Columbus Dictionary   1

Preface

This dictionary began in the 1960s with a personal desire to learn about Columbus and his milieu. As it gradually became apparent that many matters were not addressed adequately in the available biographies, I began assembling a personal Columbus bibliography based on the holdings of the various libraries I visited and keeping a personal annotation on the contents of each book and article in the bibliography. The project has resulted in both *A Columbus Dictionary* and the parallel publication, sponsored jointly by Omnigraphics, Inc., and the John Carter Brown Library at Brown University, *Columbus: An Annotated Guide to the Scholarship on His Life and Writings* (Detroit: Omnigraphics, 1991).

In pursuit of these two projects, I have visited and used the collections of the following libraries: the Biblioteca Civica Berio in Genoa; the library of the University of Genoa; the Biblioteca Nacional in Madrid; the various libraries at Brown University, including the John Carter Brown and Rockefeller Libraries; the Widener and Pusey Libraries at Harvard; the Stirling and Mudd Libraries at Yale; the New York Public Library; the library of the Knights of Columbus in New Haven, Connecticut; the library of the Hispanic Society of America in New York; the libraries of the State University of New York (SUNY) at Stony Brook and Albany; the libraries of the University of Michigan at Ann Arbor, including the William L. Clements Library and the Harlan Hatcher Graduate Library; the library of the University of Illinois at Urbana; the Duquesne University Library; the Hillman Library and Darlington Room Library at the University of Pittsburgh; the Pattee Library at Pennsylvania State University; the Troy H. Middleton Library at Louisiana State University; and the Suzzallo Library at the University of Washington, Seattle.

Many books and articles that I discovered with the help of the National Union

Catalogue, the Online Computer Library Center (OCLC), and the Research Libraries Information Network (RLIN) were sent to me from various other libraries and collections through interlibrary loan. The Library of Congress also furnished much valuable information and material.

I am indebted to Frederick G. Ruffner of Omnigraphics, Inc., and Robert Tolf of the Phileas Society, who commissioned me to complete *A Columbus Dictionary* for publication; to Frank Abate and the entire staff of Omnigraphics, Inc.; and to the hundreds of generous librarians at the various institutions cited above who helped me to find what I needed.

Foster Provost
Duquesne University

Introduction

Christopher Columbus (ca. 1451-1506), as every schoolchild knows, commanded the fleet of three ships—the *Niña, Pinta,* and *Santa Maria*—that has since been credited with the discovery of America. Columbus (most often referred to as CC in *A Columbus Dictionary*), however, did much more than make one famous voyage. Indeed, this great Italian navigator made four voyages to the New World while in the service of the Spanish. His relationships formed during these years; the technology and ideas evinced in his journeys; and the psychological, cultural, and spiritual attitudes reflected in his reading and his writing—his whole life, in fact—may be said to embody the spirit of the times. As such, *A Columbus Dictionary,* first of all, presents a ready reference to the people, events, circumstances, concepts, titles, objects, and so on, associated with Christopher Columbus, particularly during the years of his voyages, from 1492 to 1506. Each entry gives a succinct account of itself in relation to the navigator.

Scholars, students, and general readers may come to *A Columbus Dictionary* with questions that have been debated for years, such as, What exactly did CC discover on 12 October 1492? or, What does it mean to *discover a country*? The *Dictionary* is, therefore, also a guide for researchers of all kinds—from junior high school students to post graduates—to various sources that contain in-depth discussions of details relating to CC and his achievements. Reference notes under specific headings will guide the user to one or more passages in a standard work on Columbus and, usually, to one or more additional references. Contrasting viewpoints are presented. Furthermore, words in boldface in the text of most entries guide the reader to more information listed under those words in separate *Dictionary* entries. For example, in the text of the **papal bulls** entry, **Spain** refers the user to the entry under the latter term. Names are alphabetized by the form found in the majority of standard dictionaries and encyclopedias, with cross references included under alternate forms where appropriate. Finally, the researcher may also want to explore the author's *Columbus: An Annotated Guide to the Scholarship on His Life and Writings* (Detroit: Omnigraphics, 1991).

Because of the dearth of scholarly treatments on Columbus in English, the standard works by the American scholar Samuel Eliot Morison (1887-1976) have been critical sources for the *Dictionary*. The usual reference to a standard work at the end of an entry is to one of the following five works by Morison. Abbreviations given here are used in the references.

*AOS*1   Samuel Eliot Morison. *Admiral of the Ocean Sea: A Life of Christopher Columbus,* 2 vols. (Boston: Little, Brown, 1942). A lucid, highly readable account, with particular emphasis on the voyages, special attention to navigational matters, and extensive scholarly annotations. Most paperback two-volume editions are not reprints of *AOS*1, but of *AOS*2 with different pagination.

*AOS*2   Samuel Eliot Morison. *Admiral of the Ocean Sea: A Life of Christopher Columbus* (Boston: Little, Brown, 1942). The Pulitzer Prize-winning abridgement of *AOS*1, same title. This edition omits (1) the preliminary chapter on ships and sailing; (2) all the scholarly notes; and (3) the chapter on syphilis, *AOS*1 II 193-218. Also, each chapter is shortened.

*EDA*1   Samuel Eliot Morison. *The European Discovery of America: The Northern Voyages* (New York: Oxford University Press, 1971).

*EDA*2   Samuel Eliot Morison. *The European Discovery of America: The Southern Voyages* (New York: Oxford University Press, 1974). An abridgement of *Admiral of the Ocean Sea* with updated notes is provided on pages 3-183 and 236-71.

JOD   Samuel Eliot Morison, ed. and trans. *Journals and Other Documents on the Life and Voyages of Christopher Columbus* (New York: Heritage, 1963).

Bibliography

This reference list includes sources directly used to compile the *Dictionary* as well as a representative selection of materials covering current issues in Columbus studies. The works by Samuel Eliot Morison, cited in the Introduction, are considered the standard biographical sources.

Arens, W. *The Man-Eating Myth: Anthropology and Anthropophagy* (New York: Oxford University Press, 1979).

Axtell, James. "Europeans, Indians, and the Age of Discovery in American History Textbooks." *American Historical Review* 92 (June 1987): 621-32.

Cheyfitz, Eric. *The Poetics of Imperialism, Translation and Colonization from The Tempest to Tarzan* (New York: Oxford University Press, 1991).

Chiappelli, Fredi, ed. *First Images of America: The Impact of the New World on the Old* (Berkeley and Los Angeles: University of California Press, 1976).

Columbus, Ferdinand. *The Life of Admiral Christopher Columbus by his Son Ferdinand.* Edited and translated by Benjamin Keen (New Brunswick, NJ: Rutgers University Press, 1959).

Cook, Sherburne F., and Woodrow Borah. *Essays in Population History: Mexico and the Caribbean* (Berkeley and Los Angeles: University of California Press, 1971).

Crosby, Alfred W. *The Columbian Exchange: Biological and Cultural Consequences of 1492* (Westport, Conn.: Greenwood Press, 1972).

———. *Ecological Imperialism: The Biological Expansion of Europe, 900-1900* (Cambridge: Cambridge University Press, 1986).

Denevan, William M., ed. *The Native Population of the Americas in 1492* (Madison: University of Wisconsin Press, 1976).

De Vorsey, Louis, and John Parker, eds. *In the Wake of Columbus: Islands and Controversy* (Detroit: Wayne State University Press, 1985).

Floyd, Troy S. *The Columbian Dynasty in the Caribbean, 1492-1526* (Albuquerque: University of New Mexico Press, 1973).

Gerace, Donald T., comp. *Proceedings of the First San Salvador Conference* (Ft. Lauderdale: The College Center of the Finger Lakes Bahamian Field Station, 1987).

Hulme, Peter. *Colonial Encounters, Europe and the Native Caribbean, 1492-1797* (New York: Methuen, 1986).

Jane, Cecil, ed. *The Four Voyages of Columbus* (New York: Dover, 1988).

———, trans. *Journal of Christopher Columbus* (New York: Potter, 1960).

León-Portilla, Miguel. *Mesoamerica 1492 and on the Eve of 1992* (College Park, Md.: University of Maryland, 1988).

Madariaga, Salvador de. *Christopher Columbus* (New York: Ungar, 1967).

Major, R.H., ed. *Select Letters of Christopher Columbus, with Other Original Documents, Relating to his Four Voyages to the New World* (New York: Corinth, 1961).

Martínez-Hidalgo, José María. *Columbus's Ships.* Edited by Howard I. Chapelle (Barre, MA: Barre Publishers, 1966).

Merriman, R.B. *The Rise of the Spanish Empire in the Old World and the New* (New York: Macmillan, 1936).

"Columbus and the New World." *National Geographic Magazine* 170 (November 1986): 566-99.

O'Gorman, Edmundo. *The Invention of America: An Inquiry into the Historical Nature of the New World and the Meaning of its History* (Bloomington: Indiana University Press, 1961).

Pagden, Anthony. *Spanish Imperialism and the Political Imagination* (New Haven: Yale University Press, 1990).

Parry, J.H. *The Discovery of the Sea* (New York: Dial Press, 1974).

Provost, Foster. *Columbus: An Annotated Guide to the Scholarship on His Life and Writings, 1750-1988* (Detroit: Omnigraphics, Inc., 1991).

Sale, Kirkpatrick. *The Conquest of Paradise: Christopher Columbus and the Columbian Legacy* (New York: Knopf, 1990).

Sauer, Carl Ortwin. *The Early Spanish Main* (Berkeley and Los Angeles: University of California Press, 1966).

Schwartz, Stuart B. *The Iberian Mediterranean and Atlantic Traditions in the Formation of Columbus as a Colonizer* (Minneapolis: University of Minnesota Press, 1986).

Stevens-Arroyo, Antonio M. *Cave of the Jagua: The Mythological World of the Tainos* (Albuquerque: University of New Mexico Press, 1988).

Sweet, Leonard I. "Christopher Columbus and the Millennial Vision of the New World." *Catholic Historical Review* 72 (July 1986): 369-82.

Taviani, Paolo Emilio. *Christopher Columbus: The Grand Design* (London: Orbis, 1985).

Todorov, Tzvetan. *The Conquest of America: The Question of the Other.* Translated by Richard Howard (New York: Harper & Row, 1984).

Vargas Llosa, Mario. "Questions of Conquest: What Columbus Wrought, and What He Did Not." *Harper's Magazine* 281 (December 1990): 45-53.

Viola, Herman J., and Carolyn Margolis, eds. *Seeds of Change: A Quincentennial Commemoration* (Washington and London: Smithsonian Institution Press, 1991).

Washburn, Wilcomb E. "The Meaning of 'Discovery' in the Fifteenth and Sixteenth Centuries," *American Historical Review* 68 (October 1962): 1-21.

Watts, Pauline Moffitt. "Prophecy and Discovery: On the Spiritual Origins of Christopher Columbus's 'Enterprise of the Indies'," *American Historical Review* 90 (February 1985): 73-102.

A

ACKLIN ISLAND

An island in the **Bahamas** southeast of **San Salvador Island** (formerly, Watlings Island) at twenty-two degrees North **latitude** and seventy-four degrees West **longitude.** Here, according to S.E. Morison's analysis of CC's *Journal of the First Voyage*, CC expected to find "the king who owned so many golden vessels." Morison places CC in the area west of Acklin from 20 to 24 October 1492.

Ref. *AOS1* I, 326-28; *AOS2*, 49; *JOD*, 76-81.

ACUL BAY

A sheltered bay on the northwest shore of **Haiti,** discovered by CC on 20 December 1492. CC sent men to visit the nearby **Taino Indian** village and remarked on what he perceived as the pristine innocence and generosity of the inhabitants.

Ref. *AOS1* I, 379-83; *AOS2*, 293-97.

ADELANTADO

A title combining both military and civil functions, used in the **Canary Islands** to designate the governor of a province that was being conquered. CC conferred this title on his brother **Bartholomew Columbus** and the Spanish sovereigns confirmed it. Bartholomew, as adelantado, presided over the settlement and conquest of **Hispaniola** during CC's absence between the **Second** and **Third Voyages** from 1496 to 1498.

Ref. *AOS1* II, 164; Aldo Albonico, "Bartolomeo Colombo, adelantado mayor de las Indias," *Presenza Italiana in Andalusia II* (Bologna: Cappelli, 1986), 51-70.

ADMIRAL OF THE OCEAN

The title awarded to Columbus in the **Capitulations of 1492,** modeled on the title and office of the Almirante Mayor of **Castile.** The position carried with it jurisdiction over Spanish ships and their crews bound for CC's discoveries from the time they crossed the meridian of the westernmost **Azores,** until they crossed back over the same meridian on the return voyage. This authority was voided in 1500. The title was hereditary and passed to CC's son **Diego Columbus** when the mariner died.

Ref. *AOS1* I, 95-96, II, 19-21; *AOS2*, 365-67; Florentino Pérez Embid, "El Almirantazgo de

Castilla, hasta las Capitulaciones de Santa Fé,'' *Anuario de Estudios Americanos* (Seville) 1 (1944): 1-170.

AENEAS SYLVIUS
See **SYLVIUS, AENEAS.**

AETERNI REGIS
See **PAPAL BULLS.**

AFONSO V (1432-1481)
King of Portugal, of the House of Avis (1438-1481). Afonso, nephew of Prince **Henry the Navigator** and father of **John II,** occupied the Portuguese throne when CC first arrived in **Lisbon** in the summer of 1476, and when **Spain** and **Portugal** signed the **Treaty of Alcáçovas** in 1479.

Ref. *Encyclopedia Britannica,* 11th ed., s.v. ''Portugal.''

AGUADO, JUAN (n.d.)
The captain of a **ship** in the fleet that CC commanded on the **Second Voyage** in 1493. He returned to **Spain** with **Antonio de Torres.** On 5 August 1495 he sailed from **Seville** with a commission from the Spanish sovereigns to investigate and report on CC's conduct as viceroy and governor. CC, who was absent from **Isabela** when Aguado arrived in October, was warned by a message from his **adelantado (Bartholomew Columbus),** and returned to find Aguado assuming the functions of viceroy and taking evidence. CC treated Aguado patiently but promptly resolved to return to **Castille,** which he did in

March 1496 to protect his interests against the report forthcoming from Aguado.

Ref. *AOS*1 II, 56, 175-76; *AOS*2, 396, 493-94; Guillermo Esteves Völkers, *Appendice al Tarjeto Histórico* (Madrid: privately published, 1964), 431; Guillermo Esteves Völkers, *Tarjetero histórico: Noticias sobre el segundo viaje del Almirante d. Cristóbal Colón* (Madrid: privately published, 1960), 656.

AGUJA
The only **caravel** to reach **Spain** in the fleet of 30 vessels that departed from **Santo Domingo** about 30 June 1502, carrying **Francisco de Bobadilla** and 200,000 castellanos' worth of **gold,** an enormous amount. Defying CC's warnings of an approaching **hurricane,** the governor, **Ovando,** dispatched the fleet. It was immediately struck by a hurricane at the eastern end of **Hispaniola.** Among those lost were CC's friend **Antonio de Torres,** commanding the **ship** carrying Bobadilla and the **cacique Guarionex.** Ironically, the *Aguja* bore a generous shipment of gold, 4000 pesos, for CC. This actually reached **Diego Columbus** and became part of CC's considerable estate.

Ref. *AOS*1 II, 325; *AOS*2, 590.

AILLY, PIERRE D'
See **D'AILLY, PIERRE.**

ALCÁÇOVAS, TREATY OF

The treaty of 1479 in which **Portugal** conceded **Spain**'s right to the **Canary Islands** and Spain conceded to Portugal exclusive rights to the African coast and islands south of the Canaries. The treaty was confirmed by Sixtus IV's **papal bull** *Aeterni Regis* in 1481.

> Ref. *AOS*1 I, 52, 427, 439; *AOS*2, 40, 344; Edward Gaylord Bourne, "The History and Determination of the Line of Demarcation Established by Pope Alexander VI, between the Spanish and Portuguese Fields of Discovery and Colonization," *Yale Review* 1 (1892): 35-55.

ALEXANDER VI (1431-1503)

Pope (1492-1503). Born Rodrigo Llancol in 1431 at Xativa, **Spain,** near Valencia, he assumed the maternal surname of Borgia when his maternal uncle became pope as Calixtus III in 1455. He studied law at Bologna and, after his uncle's elevation, became successively bishop, cardinal, and vice-chancellor of the Church. Borgia served in the Curia under five popes. He was also the father of Cesare (b. 1476) and Lucrezia Borgia (b. 1480).

Under the influence of King **Ferdinand,** whose aid had helped him rise in the Catholic Church, Alexander VI issued five bulls on the new discoveries favorable to Spain vis-à-vis **Portugal.** The third of these bulls, *Inter Caetera II* (1493; *see* **Carvajal, Bernardino de**), drew the famous **demarcation line** one hundred leagues west of the **Azores,** which divided both western and eastern discoveries between Portugal and Spain, and negated the Portuguese interpretation of the earlier bull, *Aeterni Regis* (Pope Sixtus IV, 1481) which, according to the Portuguese, gave them rights of discovery to everything south of the **Canary Islands.** The north-south line was fixed by the Treaty of Tordesillas at forty-three degrees thirty minutes West **longitude.** *See* **PAPAL BULLS.**

> Ref. Edward Gaylord Bourne, "The History and Determination of the Line of Demarcation Established by Pope Alexander VI, between the Spanish and Portuguese Fields of Discovery and Colonization," *Yale Review* 1 (1892): 35-55; *Encyclopedia Britannica,* 11th ed., s.v. "Alexander"; H. Van der Linden, "Alexander VI and the Demarcation of the Maritime and Colonial Domains of Spain and Portugal, 1493-1494," *American Historical Review* 22 (1916-17): 1-20.

ALHANDRA

A town in **Portugal** on the northwest bank of the **Tagus River** at the beginning of the estuary. It lies down the slope from the **Convento de San Antonio de Castanheira,** where the queen, **Doña Leonor,** was residing when CC returned from the **Indies** in March 1493. CC visited her at this monastery before departing for **Palos,** after he visited King **John II.**

Ref. _AOS_1 I, 443-46; _AOS_2, 348-49.

ALIXANDRE, FRAY (n.d.)

The chaplain on board the _Vizcaina,_ one of the four **caravels** that constituted the fleet on CC's **Fourth Voyage.**

Ref. _AOS_1 II, 321, 336; Consuelo Varela, "El rol del cuarto viaje colombino," _Anuario de Estudios Americanos_ (Seville) 42 (1985): 243-95.

ALTA VELA

An isolated rock that lies just south of the southernmost point of **Hispaniola,** midway between the east and west extremities of the island. It lies just west of **Beata Island,** CC's **landfall** on the **Third Voyage,** 1498.

Ref. _AOS_1 II, 157, 287, 327; _AOS_2, 477, 560, 592.

AMERICA

This name is commonly attributed to **Martin Waldseemüller,** who gave the name to South America on his world map in 1507. Recent speculation on the subject suggests that the term might have resulted when **Amerigo Vespucci's** name was conflated with a tribal name resembling "America" in Brazil.

Ref. Harold Jantz, "Images of America in the German Renais-sance," _First Images of America,_ vol. 1, ed. Fred Chiapelli (Berkeley: University of California Press, 1976), 91-106, esp. 96-100; Carlos Sanz, _El nombre América: libros y mapas que lo impusieron_ (Madrid: Suarez, 1959).

AMPOLLETA

Also called _reloj de arena._ A sand-clock or half-hour glass used to keep time on voyages in CC's day. The **gromet,** or ship's boy on duty in each watch, was assigned to reverse the ampolleta as soon as the sand ran out.

Ref. _AOS_1 I, 220-22.

ANACOANA (d. ca. 1503)

Became the most powerful **cacique** of **Xaragua** in **Hispaniola** when her brother **Behechio** was slain by the Spanish. She had moved from Maguana to Xaragua to live with her brother when her husband **Caonabó** died while a prisoner on board the _India._ **Nicolas de Ovando,** convinced that Anacoana planned a conspiracy against his rule, lured her along with many of her fellow Xaraguans to a festival, during which his men massacred some Xaraguans, burned others alive, and took Anacoana to **Santo Domingo.** There she was "tried" for insurrection and hanged. Sources differ as to the possibility of the existence of such a plot to overthrow Ovando.

Ref. _AOS_1 II, 295, 397; Bartolomé de Las Casas, _Popery Truly Display'd in Its Bloody Colours; or_

A Faithful Narrative of the Horrid and Unexampled Massacres, Butcheries, and All Manner of Cruelties, That Hell and Malice Could Invent, Committed by the Popish Spanish Party on the Inhabitants of West-India. . . . (London: R. Hewson, 1689), 10-11.

ANJOU, RENÉ D'
See **RENÉ D'ANJOU.**

ANTIGUA

An island north of **Guadeloupe** and northeast of **Montserrat**. It was discovered and named "Santa María la Antigua" by CC on his **Second Voyage** in November 1493.

Ref. *AOS*1 II, 73; *AOS*2, 410.

ANTILLES

Also known as Antilhas; the name given on the Cantino map (**Lisbon,** 1502) to the **West Indies.** It was adopted by the early sixteenth-century Portuguese historian **João de Barros** and later, to some extent, by the Spanish who called the Caribbean Sea "El Mar de las Antillas." The name was undoubtedly derived from the mythical island **Antillia.**

Ref. *AOS*1 I, 442.

ANTILLIA

Before CC's voyages, many mythical islands were actually thought to exist in the Atlantic. Antillia was the most frequently spoken of by scholars such as **Paolo del Pozzo Toscanelli.** It was said to be the largest of these islands.

Ref. W.H. Babcock, "Antillia and the Antilles," *Geographical Review* 9 (1920): 109-24; Armando Cortesão, *The Nautical Chart of 1424 and the Early Discovery and Cartographical Representation of America* (Coimbra, Portugal: University of Coimbra, 1954); G.R. Crone, "The Origin of the Name 'Antillia'," *Geographical Journal* (London) 91 (1938): 260-61.

ARAGÓN

The former kingdom in the **Iberian Peninsula** extending from the Mediterranean west to the kingdom of **Castile,** and bounded on the south by **Granada.** When CC arrived in **Spain** in 1485, Aragón, under King **Ferdinand V,** had recently been combined with the kingdom of Castile, under Queen **Isabel I,** to form the kingdom of Spain. As the larger region, Castile dominated the new kingdom, and, as the western region with natural interests in the Atlantic, it dominated the pioneering and conquest of the **New World.** Castilian was the dominant literary and diplomatic language of the Iberian Peninsula and became the prestige language of Spain.

Ref. R.B. Merriman, *The Rise of the Spanish Empire in the Old World and the New,* vol. 1 (New York: Macmillan, 1936).

ARANA
See **HARANA.**

ARAWAK
A term that refers both to **Indians** living in South **America** and to a group of Indian languages spoken by the native Caribbeans. *See also* **TAINO INDIANS.**

ARCHIVE OF THE INDIES
This massive collection of mostly unpublished and unresearched documents accumulated at the **Casa de Contratación** in **Seville** over the course of several centuries of administration of the Spanish empire overseas. The collection is still housed in the building constructed for the Casa de Contratación and remains the chief resource for historical study of the entire Spanish activity in the **New World.**

> Ref. M. Romero Tallafigo, ''El archivo general de las Indias: acceso a las fuentes documentales sobre Andalucía y América en el siglo XVI,'' *Andalucía y América en el Siglo XVI. Actas de las II Jornadas de Andalucía y América,* vol. 1 (Seville: Escuela de Estudios Hispano-Americanos, 1983), 455-84.

ARROW, CAPE OF THE
See **FLECHA, CABO DE LA.**

ARROWS, THE
See **FLECHAS, LAS.**

ARZILA
A Portuguese fortress on the coast of Morocco sixty-five miles from **Cádiz.** When CC began his **Fourth Voyage** in 1502, he stopped here to help the Portuguese raise a Moorish siege. By 13 May, when CC arrived at Arzila with his four **ships,** the **Moors** had already left and CC proceeded to the **Canary Islands.**

> Ref. *AOS*1 II, 323; *AOS*2, 588.

ASSERETO DOCUMENT
The Genoese court document recording a sworn deposition by CC on 25 August 1479. The deposition describes CC's part in a dispute between **Ludovico Centurione** and **Paolo di Negro** concerning payment for an order of sugar that CC was unable to purchase in **Funchal, Madeira.** Di Negro had not given CC all of the money that Centurione claimed he had sent to di Negro for this purpose. The document is critical to CC's biography because it places his birth in the year 1451.

> Ref. *AOS*1 I, 30-31, 49; Ugo Assereto, ''La data della nascità di Colombo accertata da un documento nuovo,'' *Giornale Storico e Letterario Liguriano* (Genoa) 5 (1904): 5-16, a copy of an original document; *JOD,* 8-9.

ASTROLABE
A mariner's instrument for finding **latitude** by the elevation of a star. CC took one on his **First Voyage** but was unable to use it. There is no evidence of his taking one on any other voy-

ages except the **Fourth.** The only instrument of celestial **navigation** that CC employed was the marine **quadrant;** this, however, he never learned to use accurately until he spent a year in **Jamaica,** where the pitch of the ship did not throw him off.

Ref. *AOS*2, 184, 319.

ASUNCIÓN, ISLA DE LA
In August 1498, the name CC gave to one of three small islands just north of the "Bocas," or mouths, of the **Orinoco River.**

Ref. *AOS*1 II, 276-77.

AZAMBUJA, DIOGO D'
See **D'AZAMBUJA, DIOGO.**

AZORES
A chain of islands 700-1000 miles west of **Portugal** discovered by **Henry the Navigator**'s mariners while looking for **St. Brendan's Island.** Seven of the Azores had been discovered by 1439; **Flores** and **Corvo,** the farthest west, were discovered in 1452 by **Diogo de Teive.** CC anchored the *Niña* at **Santa Maria** in February 1493 on the first return voyage and nearly lost a large part of his crew as prisoners to the Portuguese captain of the island, **João de Castanheira,** who was hostile toward the Spanish.

Ref. *AOS*1 I, 39-431, II, 185-88; *AOS*2, 29, 57, 60-66, 322-26.

AZUA, PUERTO VIEJO DE
The landlocked harbor at the head of Ocoa Bay on the south coast of **Hispaniola** where CC's fleet made their rendezvous after being separated in the **hurricane** of about July 1502; it was this **storm** which sank the fleet carrying **Bobadilla** back toward **Spain.** *See* AGUJA.

Ref. *AOS*1 II, 327, 396; *AOS*2, 592, 649.

B

BABEQUE

The name attributed to an island north of **Cuba** by Cuban natives whom CC and his party met in November 1492. S.E. Morison identifies the island as **Great Inagua,** about eighty miles northeast of the easternmost point of Cuba. It was discovered by **Martín Alonso Pinzón** in the *Pinta* on the **First Voyage.**

Ref. *AOS*1 I, 343-78 *passim; AOS*2, 262.

BAHAMA ISLANDS

An archipelago of some 3000 islands, islets, and cays in the Atlantic Ocean extending about 600 miles, from a point about fifty miles southeast of the Florida Keys, almost to **Haiti.** CC's first **landfall** was in the Bahamas at the island of **Guanahani,** which CC renamed **San Salvador.** One of the most persistent controversies concerning CC's career centers on which of these islands is the site of the first landfall. Many Bahamian Islands have been identified as Guanahani, most frequently Watlings (now officially San Salvador), followed by **Grand Turk** and **Samana Cay.**

BANK OF ST. GEORGE

The commercial bank in **Genoa** long associated with the Genoese commonwealth. CC held the bank in great respect and sent it a copy of his *Book of Privileges* for safekeeping. When he had become economically successful, CC sent a letter to the bank offering a sum of money to be distributed to the citizens of Genoa, but apparently the bank never responded.

Ref. G. Giacchero, "Colombo e i suoi rapporti col Banco di San Giorgio," *Bol Civico Ist Col* (Genoa) 1 (1955): 19-27; Henry Harrisse, *Christopher Columbus and the Bank of St. George* (New York: privately published, 1888).

BARACOA

The first Spanish settlement in **Cuba,** it was founded in 1512 on a site first visited by CC on 27 November 1492. Baracoa lies on the northeast coast of Cuba in **Oriente Province** and is the largest **New World** town on the route of CC's **First Voyage.**

Ref. *AOS*1 I, 156, 359-62; *AOS*2, 274-78.

BARCELONA

The great Catalonian port where the itinerant monarchs **Isabel** and **Ferdinand** received CC in the Plaza de los Reyes between 15 and 20 April 1493, on his return from discovering the **West Indies.** The unparalleled accolade received by CC, including the privilege of sitting down in the presence of the monarchs, entertainment by the Cardinal of **Spain, Don Pedro Gonzales de Mendoza,** and the quick approval of a second fleet of discovery, constituted the high point of the navigator's career. The first printed version of CC's **Letter to Santangel,** dispatched from **Lisbon** on 4 March 1492, bore his announcement of the discovery and his description of the **Bahamas** and West Indies and was published in Barcelona. This letter, one of the most widely published documents of the time, made CC an instant sensation throughout Europe.

Barcelona was the site of the first outbreak of **syphilis** in the spring of 1493, an epidemic that spread through Europe in the following years. The disease is considered by many scholars to have been brought from the newly discovered islands by the natives who returned with CC or by Spanish sailors infected while they were in the West Indies.

Ref. *AOS*1 II, 4-26, 203-5; *AOS*2, 203-10.

BARIAY, BAHÍA

This bay on the northeast coast of Cuba is presumably the same bay that Columbus called "San Salvador." CC entered the bay with his fleet on 28 November 1492 after sailing through the **Bahamas** from **Guanahani.** Bahía Bariay is in sight of La Teta de Bariay, a mountain whose shape corresponds to the mountain described by CC from his position in the harbor San Salvador.

Ref. *AOS*1 I, 330-37; *AOS*2, 253-55.

BARROS, JOÃO DE (1496-1570)

The historian known as the "Portuguese Livy" who, in his *Decades of Asia* (begun 1539, published 1552), gives an account of CC's negotiations with **John II** for a fleet of discovery that would sail west to the **Indies.** Barros, calling CC a Genoese, says that King John and his geographical committee looked on CC as a vain boaster full of myths derived largely from **Marco Polo.**

Ref. *AOS*1 I, 93-94; *AOS*2, 70-72.

BASTIDAS, RODRIGO DE (b. ca. 1460)

A Spanish mariner who sailed west from **Venezuela** to the Gulf of Darien in **Panama** before CC's voyage to Panama in 1502. **Alonso de Hojeda,** an infamous adventurer and sometime pirate, claimed that he and Bastidas had reached Retrete in Panama before CC, but the balance of evidence seems to be against this claim.

Ref. *AOS1* II, 313-14.

BATABANÓ, GULF OF
A fishing port in southern **Cuba** near San Cristóbal de la Habana, a town founded in 1514 on the south coast on the bay Ensenada Broa. CC appears to have anchored near here in late May 1494 during the **Second Voyage** while exploring the **Queen's Garden.** Near this anchorage, according to the reports of the voyage, a strange incident occurred in which several light-complexioned men in white tunics appeared with a band of natives and chased away a Spanish bowman who had gone ashore to look for game. CC associated these men in white with **Prester John.**

Ref. *AOS1* I, 461-65; *AOS2*, 461-65.

BAY ISLANDS
Also called Islas de la Bahía. A group of small islands off the coast of **Honduras** through which CC sailed on his way toward **Panama** on the **Fourth Voyage.** CC stopped at the island of **Bonacca.**

Ref. *AOS1* II, 328.

BAYONA
A port in **Galicia,** northwestern **Spain,** just north of the Portuguese border. **Martín Alonso Pinzón,** commanding the *Pinta,* made his European landfall here near the end of the **First Voyage,** presumably a few days before CC, commanding the *Niña,* reached **Restelo** in **Portugal,** just below **Lisbon** on the estuary of the **Tagus River.** Like CC, Pinzón proceeded from the point of his landfall to **Palos.** He arrived on 15 March 1493, a few hours after CC.

Ref. *AOS1* II, 3-4; Ana María Manzano Fernández-Heredia and Juan Manzano Manzano, *Los Pinzones y el descubrimiento de América,* vol. 1 (Madrid: Ediciones Cultural Hispánica, 1988).

BEATA ISLAND
An island off the southern coast of **Hispaniola** just east of **Alta Vela** and about 100 miles west of **Santo Domingo.** It was CC's **landfall** on the **Third Voyage,** 19 August 1498. On the **Second Voyage** CC called it "Catalina," but on the **Third Voyage** he gave it the name "Beata."

Ref. *AOS1* II, 157, 287-88, 327, 409; *AOS2*, 477, 560, 592, 658.

BEAUJEU, ANNE OF (1460-1522)
The elder daughter of Louis XI of France and regent of France during the minority of her younger brother **Charles VIII. Bartholomew Columbus** attached himself to her household when he went to France to try to sell CC's **Enterprise of the Indies.**

Ref. *AOS1* I, 119, II, 163.

BECHALLA

A Flemish ship, one of a Genoese convoy that passed through the Strait of Gibraltar in August 1476 carrying merchandise, probably chiefly **mastic,** to be sold in **Portugal, England,** and Flanders. When a group of French corsairs attacked the convoy off **Cape St. Vincent** at the southwest corner of Portugal, the *Bechalla* was sunk in the ensuing battle. Some scholars believe that CC was on board and that he swam ashore near **Lagos** in Portugal.

> Ref. *AOS1* I, 31-32; *AOS2*, 23-24; Giuseppe Pessagno, "Questioni Colombiane," *Atti Società Liguriana della Storia Patria* (Genoa) 53 (1926): 539-641.

BEHAIM, MARTIN (ca. 1459-ca. 1507)

A German from Nuremberg who claimed, perhaps fraudulently, to be a student of **Regiomontanus** and successfully entered the courtly circle in **Portugal.** King **John II** appointed him to his maritime commission and knighted him in 1485. In 1492, in Nuremberg, he constructed a famous globe mentioned in the *Nuremberg Chronicle,* whose features reflect geographical ideas markedly similar to those of CC. There is no proof, however, that the two men knew each other.

> Ref. *AOS1* I, 88-89, 99-101; *AOS2*, 66-68, 76-78; Arthur Davies, "Behaim, Martellus and Columbus," *Geographical Journal* (London) 143 (1977): 451-59; E.G. Ravenstein, *Martin Behaim, His Life, and His Globe* (London: Philip, 1908).

BEHECHIO (d. ca. 1502)

The **cacique** of **Xaragua** at the time of the **Roldán** revolt against CC in **Hispaniola.** He was the brother of **Anacoana,** the wife of **Caonabó,** both of whom were powerful caciques. Behechio was killed by the Spanish.

> Ref. *AOS1* II, 172, 295-96.

BELÉN

The name given by CC to a river (Indian name "Yebra" or "Gieura") on the Caribbean coast of **Panama** where CC's fleet anchored for three and a half months in early 1503 during the **Fourth Voyage.** After searching unsuccessfully for **gold** and an abortive attempt to establish a colony here at a site he called Santa María de Belén, CC concluded his explorations, abandoned one of his worm-eaten **ships,** and sailed back toward **Hispaniola.** He ultimately beached his two remaining ships on **Jamaica,** where he remained for a year until his rescue in June 1504.

> Ref. *AOS1* II, 366-76; *AOS2*, 622-32.

BERARDI, JUANOTO (d. 1495)

A Florentine merchant in **Seville** and friend of CC, he provided active support for both the **First Voyage** and the **Second.** Berardi formed a business partnership with CC to handle the traffic to the **Indies** and, in this capacity, he financed the first trip of **Bartholomew Columbus** to the **New World** in 1494. Berardi put so many of his resources into the partnership that his other business interests were ruined. Berardi died in December 1495 just before the disastrous loss of a fleet he had financed for Columbus left his estate in bankruptcy.

Ref. *AOS2*, 104; Consuelo Varela, *Colón y los florentinos* (Madrid: Alianza, 1988); Consuelo Varela, ''Florentines' Friendship and Kinship with Christopher Columbus,'' *Proceedings of the First San Salvador Conference: Columbus and His World,* comp. Donald T. Gerace (Ft. Lauderdale: The College Center of the Finger Lakes Bahamian Field Station, 1987), 33-43.

BERGANTIN

A sailboat of moderate size, equipped with oars, which was used by the Spanish in the Caribbean. CC planned to use such boats to capture the hostile **Carib Indians** to sell as **slaves** in **Spain.** The project was vetoed by Queen **Isabel.**

Ref. *AOS1* II, 178, 317.

BERMUDA
See SANTIAGO DE PALOS.

BERMÚDEZ, FRANCISCO (n.d.)
The owner of the *Santiago de Palos*, a **caravel** of the **Fourth Voyage,** nicknamed *Bermuda* for its owner.

Ref. *AOS1* II, 228.

BERNAL (n.d.)
A Valencian apothecary and crew member on the **Fourth Voyage,** Bernal led one of the revolts against CC's authority while the expedition was waiting to be rescued in **Jamaica** in the spring of 1504. His revolt was terminated by the coming of a **caravel** commanded by **Diego de Escobar. Ovando,** governor of **Santo Domingo,** on learning of CC's misfortune, had sent the caravel from **Hispaniola** not to rescue the crew but, apparently, merely to scout CC's situation.

Ref. *AOS1* II, 407-8.

BERNÁLDEZ, ANDRÉS (ca. 1450-ca. 1513)
The curate of Los Palacios and chaplain to the Archbishop of **Seville.** CC visited him while in Seville after the **Second Voyage** and deposited the journals of this voyage with him. Bernáldez used these and other documents that CC left with him to write the *Historia de los Reyes Católicos.* Bernáldez describes the elaborate golden jewelry that CC displayed with his captive **Indians,** making them wear it for the Spanish sovereigns at the court at Almazán, north of Ma-

drid. Bernáldez notes CC's conviction that the eastern tip of **Cuba** was the easternmost point of the Eurasian land mass and records the navigator's enthusiasm for the beauty of **Jamaica.** Bernáldez's account is the chief source of information on the exploration of Cuba on the Second Voyage.

Ref. *AOS1* II, 119-50, 123-56, 125, 221-23; *AOS2*, 447-61, 474-76, 505-7; Andrés Bernáldez, *Historia de los Reyes Católicos D. Fernando y Da. Isabel,* vol. 1 (Granada: Zamora, 1856).

BIBLIOTECA COLOMBINA

The remains of the library of **Ferdinand Columbus,** numbering 4231 volumes in his own catalog (see reference note below). The collection holds the surviving books that were owned by CC containing the admiral's marginal notes or **postils.** An excellent nineteenth-century catalog provides a guide to the books although, as this dictionary is being readied for press, the books are boxed and waiting for housing as a result of the recent collapse of the library roof. Traditionally, the Biblioteca Colombina is housed in the cathedral at **Seville.**

Ref. Servando Arboli Faraudo, *Biblioteca Colombina, Catalogo de sus libros impresos de la santa metropolitana y patriarcal iglesia de Sevilla,* 7 vols. (Seville: E. Rasco, 1888-94). This describes the surviving collection; for Ferdi-nand Columbus's own catalog of the library in its early state, see the facsimile of the manuscript in the Colombiana collection, A.M. Huntington, *Catalogue of the Library of Ferdinand Columbus* (New York: privately published, 1905).

BISSIPART, GEORGES
See **COLOMBO JUNIOR.**

BOBADILLA, BEATRIZ DE
See **MOYA, MARQUESA DE.**

BOBADILLA, FRANCISCO DE (d. 1502)
The man appointed by King **Ferdinand** and Queen **Isabel** in the spring of 1499 to go to **Hispaniola** as chief justice and royal commissioner to adjust grievances among the restless colonists. Bobadilla's departure was delayed until July 1500. He arrived in Hispaniola on 23 August while CC was away from **Santo Domingo** putting down the rebellion of **Adrian deo Moxica.** Offended by the sight of seven Spanish rebels' corpses on the gallows, Bobadilla arrested CC's brother, Don **Diego Colombo,** took over the citadel and CC's house, put Don Diego in irons, and did the same with CC when he returned. On CC's advice **Bartholomew Colombus** also surrendered, and all three were returned to **Spain** for trial by the sovereigns; this return ended the **Third Voyage.** Bobadilla's unlimited powers were conferred on him before Ferdinand and Isabel knew that CC and **Roldán** had come to terms, and when they suspected CC of weakness

in dealing with rebellions against their authority and his.

Bobadilla was on board the flagship of the fleet that sailed from Santo Domingo in the summer of 1502 despite CC's warning to the governor, **Ovando,** of an impending **hurricane.** Ovando dispatched the fleet, which was destroyed by the hurricane. One **caravel** survived, the *Aguja*, which reached Spain. Bobadilla's ship was lost with all hands.

Ref. *AOS1* II, 302-25; *AOS2*, 570-72, 577, 581, 590; J. Marino Incháustegui Cabral, ''Entorno a uno de los mas tragicos episodios de la vida de Colón,'' *Anuario de Estudios Americanos* (Seville) 24 (1967): 839-49.

BOBADILLA Y PERAZA, BEATRIZ DE (OF GOMERA) (n.d.)

A remarkably vigorous and cruel woman, noted for her beauty, who ruled the island of **Gomera** in the **Canary Islands** at the time of CC's first two voyages. A cousin and namesake of Queen **Isabel**'s good friend Beatriz de Bobadilla, the **Marquesa de Moya,** she had been a maid of honor to Queen Isabel and, later, became King **Ferdinand**'s mistress. Isabel disposed of her by marrying her to Hernán de Peraza, the captain of Gomera, who thus escaped punishment for killing a royal representative in the Canaries. In 1492, as guardian of her son, Beatriz de Peraza became *de facto* ruler of Gomera after her husband died in an island revolt. CC, who may have known her in **Spain** at some point, visited her in Gomera during the **First Voyage;** according to CC's boyhood acquaintance **Michele de Cuneo,** the widower CC was in love with her when the fleet visited Gomera during the **Second Voyage.** Nothing came of this, however, since, while CC was concerned with the occupation of **Hispaniola,** Beatriz married Alonso de Lugo, the conqueror of the important island of **Tenerife** and the first **adelantado** mayor of the Canaries.

Ref. *AOS1* I, 212-15; *AOS2*, 162-65; R.B. Merriman, *The Rise of the Spanish Empire in the Old World and the New,* vol. 2 (New York: Macmillan, 1936), chap. 16 *passim;* Antonio Rumeu de Armas, ''Cristóbal Colón y Beatriz de Bobadilla en las antevísperas del descubrimiento,'' *El Museo Canario* (Las Palmas) 75 and 76 (1960): 255-79.

BOCA DE LA SIERPE
See **SIERPE, BOCA DE LA.**

BOCAS DEL DRAGON
See **DRAGON, BOCAS DEL.**

BOHIO
The **Arawak** word for house. While in **Cuba** on the **First Voyage,** CC misunderstood the word to mean **Haiti.**

Ref. *AOS1* I, 327; *AOS2*, 250.

BONACCA

Also known as Guanaja. One of the **Bay Islands** off **Honduras**. CC landed here on the **Fourth Voyage** en route from **Hispaniola** to **Panama** and encountered a large, twenty-five person **canoe** carrying a cargo of shawls, **cotton** shirts, wooden swords with flint edges and so on, products probably of Honduran Mayan manufacture. CC took the commander of the boat captive and used him as an interpreter.

Ref. *AOS1* II, 228-33; *AOS2*, 593-95.

BOOK OF PRIVILEGES

A compendium of the various royal concessions to CC in the years 1492 to 1498, originally compiled by CC in 1497/98 before he left on the **Third Voyage.** CC, enormously proud of the concessions and undoubtedly afraid they might be compromised, had the compendium magnificently bound. One copy went to the city of **Genoa,** beyond the power of the Spanish monarchs. Three copies and a fragment are preserved: the parent Veragua Codex in the Biblioteca Nacional in Madrid; one copy of the 1502 printing in Genoa; one in Paris; one in the Library of Congress; and a fragmentary manuscript compilation at the John Carter Brown Library in Providence, Rhode Island.

The *Book of Privileges* includes (1) the **Capitulations of 1492;** (2) a series of royal cedulas and letters patent of 28 May 1493 confirming CC's titles and privileges after his return from the **First Voyage;** (3) a royal order of 16 August 1494 requiring all Spanish subjects in the **West Indies** to submit to and carry out CC's orders as admiral and viceroy; (4) a royal cedula of 23 April 1497 conceding to CC the same privileges as the admiral of **Spain;** (5) a series of royal cedulas and letters patent regarding CC's **Third Voyage** from April to December 1497; (6) a cedula confirming CC's appointment of **Bartholomew Columbus** as **adelantado** of the **Indies;** and (7) a royal confirmation of the individual concessions made to CC.

Ref. C. Pérez Bustamente, ed., *Libro de los privilegios del Almirante don Cristobal Colón (1498)* (Madrid: Real Academia de la Historia, 1951); C.L. Nichols, "The Various Forms of the Columbus Codex," *Proceedings of the Massachusetts Historical Society* 59 (1926): 148-55.

BOOK OF PROPHECIES

CC's compendium of prophetic texts, commentaries of prophecies by ancient and medieval authors, pertinent fragments of Spanish verse, and his own commentaries of these various writings. CC completed a draft of the book in the autumn of 1501; at his request, the Carthusian monk **Fray Gaspar Gorricio** read it, added some more references, and returned the manuscript to CC in March 1502. The *Book of Prophecies,* cataloged by **Ferdinand Columbus** along with the other books owned by CC, has remained in the collection in the **Biblioteca Columbina.** It has special significance as a record of CC's wide range of reading, of his genuine though limited spirituality, and of his particular concern with eschatological literature. It is an apocalyptic text that enables one to recognize the urgency of CC's sense of calling as a man chosen to penetrate the mysteries of the western ocean and reveal the lands beyond it.

Ref. Delno C. West, "Scholarly Encounters With Columbus' Libro de las Profecias," *Proceedings of the First San Salvador Conference: Columbus and His World,* comp. Donald T. Gerace (Ft. Lauderdale: The College Center of the Finger Lakes Bahamian Field Station, 1987), 45-56.

BORINQUEN
See PUERTO RICO.

BRISTOL
An important port in southwest **England,** on the Avon River, notable for its fifty-foot tides, which rival the sixty- to seventy-foot tides in the Bay of Fundy, Nova Scotia. Evidence indicates that CC might have visited Bristol as a young man. **Ferdinand Columbus** writes in the *Historie* that CC once observed fifty-foot tides in **Iceland.** Since Iceland is not noted for extreme tides, it is likely that CC had visited Bristol en route to Iceland and observed them there, and that Ferdinand erred later in his recollections. If CC went to Bristol and Iceland he probably did so in the winter of 1476/77 as a commercial agent on board a ship of the **Lisbon** office of the Genoese firm of **di Negro.** *See* NEGRO, PAOLO DI.

BUIL, FRAY BERNAL (ca. 1450-1520)
A Benedictine monk who sailed on the **Second Voyage** and a former secretary to King **Ferdinand** to whom Ferdinand and Queen **Isabel** assigned the work of converting the natives. Buil celebrated the first Mass in the **New World** on 6 January 1494, the feast of the Epiphany, at **Isabela.** He did not like CC's administrative activity and, upon his return to **Spain** in November 1494, libeled CC and declared that there was nothing of profit in **Hispaniola.** Buil was on board one of the five ships of **John Cabot**'s second voyage in 1498. His ship put into an Irish port in distress; the remaining four ships were not heard of again.

Ref. *AOS1* II, 51-115 *passim,* 166-75; *AOS2,* 397, 426, 432, 484; Fidel Fita, ed., "Fray Bernal Buyl y Cristóbal Colón: nueva colección de cartas reales, enriquecida con algunas inéditos," *Boletín de la Real Academia de la Historia* (Madrid) 18 (1891): 173-233; Fidel Fita, ed., "Fray Ber-

naldo Buyl. Documentos inéditos,''
*Boletín de la Real Academia de la
Historia* (Madrid) 22 (1893): 373-
78.

C

CABO DE LA FLECHA
See FLECHA, CABO DE LA.

CABOT, JOHN (ca. 1451-1498)
Born Giovanni Caboto in Genoa; around the age of ten taken to Venice by his father. Cabot was married and living in Venice in 1484, where he bought and sold real estate. He may have resided in Valencia in **Spain** between 1490 and 1493 and seen CC's triumphal reception in **Barcelona** in April 1493. Cabot went to **England** no later than 1495 and eventually settled with his wife and sons in **Bristol.** On 5 March 1496, he received letters-patent from **Henry VII** of England to discover and occupy lands not already known to Christians. Cabot obtained only one ship, the navicula *Matthew,* which departed Bristol about 20 May 1497. He discovered **Newfoundland** on 24 June, then sailed for Bristol around 20 July and arrived 6 August. Henry VII received Cabot at court about 10 August, gave him a reward of 10 pounds sterling, and on 13 December gave him an annuity of 20 pounds. On 3 February 1498, Cabot received letters-patent for his second voyage.

The five-ship fleet left Bristol in early May with **Fray Bernal Buil** on board. The ship bearing Fray Buil put into an Irish port in distress; the others were lost at sea.

Ref. *AOS1* I, 81, 140, II, 36-37, 271; *AOS2,* 59, 106, 379-80; *EDA1,* 157-209.

CACIQUE
Spanish rendering of the Arawak word *kaseke,* signifying the local hereditary official of native Caribbean Indians CC and his crews encountered. The caciques most known to the Spanish in **Hispaniola** in the viceroyalty included: **Guacanagarí** of Marien; **Guarionex** of Magua; **Caonabó** of Maguana; Mayobanex and Cotubanama of Higuey; **Behechio** of **Xaragua;** and **Manicaotex.**

Ref. *AOS1* II, 297; *AOS2,* 565; Kirkpatrick Sale, *The Conquest of Paradise: Christopher Columbus and the Columbian Legacy* (New York: Knopf, 1990), 99.

CÁDIZ
A port serving **Seville** with roadstead at **Sanlúcar de Barrameda,** a favorite spot for the embarkation and return of expeditions to the **West In-**

dies. CC's **Third** and **Fourth Voyages** departed from Sanlúcar. Cádiz was also the site of CC's last entry into **Spain,** at the end of the **Fourth Voyage.**

Ref. *AOS1* II, 228-33, 322, 410; *AOS2*, 514, 536, 659.

CANARY ISLANDS
An archipelago off the west coast of Africa at about twenty-eight degrees North **latitude** from which CC set sail across the Atlantic on the **First, Second,** and **Fourth Voyages.** These islands were gradually conquered by the Spanish conquistadors in the second half of the fifteenth century, in campaigns that anticipated many of the developments of the Spanish conquests in the **New World.** At the time of CC's first voyage, the main islands already under Spanish occupation were **Lanzarote,** Fuerteventura, **Gomera,** and **Ferro,** all conquered by the Herrera y Peraza family, into which **Beatriz de Bobadilla y Peraza** had married. All these islands were held by this family in an arrangement known as an hereditary captaincy, which, in 1492, Beatriz controlled as guardian for her son, the heir to the captaincy. Gran Canaria was owned directly by the crown of **Castile.** The islands of **Tenerife** and Palma were still held by aborigines in 1492, not yet conquered by the Spanish.

Ref. R.B. Merriman, *The Rise of the Spanish Empire in the Old World and the New,* vol. 2 (New York: Macmillan, 1936), chap. 16 *passim.*

CANOE
A long, narrow, dugout craft used by native Americans throughout the Caribbean area; CC introduced the word "canoa," adopted from the natives, into Spanish. Some of the canoes were reported to be large enough to hold forty to forty-five persons. CC reported one in **Jamaica** to be ninety-six feet long and eight feet at the beam. At **Bonacca Island,** CC encountered a large canoe with a waterproof, palm-leaf awning amidship.

Ref. *AOS1* I, 302-18, II, 123-24, 265, 331-32; *AOS2*, 230-31, 275-76, 451-52, 544, 594-96.

CANONIZATION
A.F.F. Roselly led a movement to canonize CC in the nineteenth century. **Bartolomé de Las Casas** destroyed any chance for this when he claimed that **Ferdinand Columbus** was CC's illegitimate son by **Beatriz Enriquez de Harana.** The refutation of the case for beatification (a step toward canonization) was made by the Italian priest Angelo Sanguineti. Roselly de Lorgues wrote a fictionalized biography which claimed that CC had married Beatriz and generally glossed over CC's many unsaintly characteristics.

Ref. A.F.F. Roselly de Lorgues, *Christophe Colomb: histoire de sa vie et de ses voyages* (Paris: Didier, 1856); Giovanni Odoardi, "Il processo di beatificazione di Cristoforo Colombo," *Studi Colombiani,* vol. 3 (Genoa: SAGA, Civico Istituto Colombiano, 1952), 261-72; Angelo Sanguineti, *La canonizzazione di Cristoforo Colombo* (Genoa: Sordo-muti, 1875).

CAONABÓ (d. 1496)

The native chieftain, **cacique** of Maguana, who may have presided over the slaughter of the Spanish garrison at **Navidad.** According to the story pieced together by **Ferdinand Columbus** and **Bartolomé de Las Casas,** Caonabó captured and killed the "**Gutiérrez** gang," who were roving the island in search of **gold** and women. He then attacked and destroyed Navidad and killed the few remaining Spaniards, driving them into the sea to drown. Later, after the Spaniards had discovered gold in **Hispaniola,** CC's captain **Hojeda** tricked Caonabó into capture and put him in the **Isabela** jail. Caonabó died at sea on board the *India* during the **ship**'s turbulent return crossing with the *Niña* from 10 March to 11 June 1496.

Ref. *AOS1* II, 91-113, 171-72, 180, 222; *AOS2,* 423-27, 433, 489-90, 496; Bartolomé de Las Casas, *Popery Truly Display'd in Its Bloody Colours; or A Faithful Narrative of the Horrid and Unexampled Massacres, Butcheries,* *and All Manner of Cruelties, That Hell and Malice Could Invent, Committed by the Popish Spanish Party on the Inhabitants of West-India.* . . . (London: R. Hewson, 1689), 9-10; Kirkpatrick Sale, *The Conquest of Paradise: Christopher Columbus and the Columbian Legacy* (New York: Knopf, 1990), 154, 166, 167.

CAPE VERDE ISLANDS

The islands off Cape Verde, the point on the west African coast where the desert ends and vegetation begins, were discovered by mariners in the service of Prince **Henry the Navigator** between 1456 and 1459. CC stopped at Boavista, Cape Verde Islands, outward bound on the **Third Voyage** in 1498 and was surprised to find the islands not green, but dry and sterile. Boavista was a leper resort where wealthy lepers hoped to be cured by eating turtle meat and drinking turtle blood. While there, CC stocked up on salted goat meat.

Ref. *AOS1* II, 237-39; *AOS2,* 29-30, 519-21.

CAPITANA

The flagship on the **Fourth Voyage.** CC and **Ferdinand Columbus** sailed on this **ship,** which was under the command of **Diego Tristan.** The ship was ultimately run ashore in **Jamaica** on 25 June 1503 to avoid sinking.

Ref. *AOS1* II, 366-75, 379-99; *AOS2,* 584-91, 639-40; José María

Martínez-Hidalgo, "Las naves de los cuatro viajes de Colón al nuevo mundo," *Temi Colombiani* (Genoa: ECIG, 1986), 201-29.

CAPITULATIONS OF 1492

The articles of agreement between CC and the Spanish sovereigns, also known as the Capitulations of Santa Fé. In five articles, each signed "It pleases their majesties, **Juan de Coloma** [the royal attorney]." Article 1: CC is appointed admiral over all islands and mainlands he discovers and the title will be hereditary; 2: CC is appointed viceroy and governor-general over the discovered islands and mainlands and may nominate three candidates to each office, from which the sovereigns will select one; 3: CC may keep one-tenth of all **gold,** silver, jewels, and merchandise produced, mined, or traded in these possessions, tax-free; 4: CC or his deputy will adjudicate disputes over these goods; 5: CC is given the option of paying one-eighth of the total expense of any ship sailing to the new possessions, and taking one-eighth of the profits.

Ref. *AOS*1 I, 138-42; *AOS*2, 104-7; Angel de Alto la guirre, "Estudio jurídico de las capitulaciones y privilegios de Cristóbal Colón," *Boletín de la Real Academia de la Historia* (Madrid) 38 (1901): 279-94; Rafael Diego Fernández, *Capitulaciones Colombinos* (Zamora, Mexico: Colegio de Mi-

choacán, 1987); Antonio Rumeu de Armas, *Nueva luz sobre las Capitulaciones de Santa Fé de 1492 concertadas entre los Reyes Católicos y Cristóbal Colón: estudio institucional y diplomático* (Madrid: Consejo Superior de Investigaciones Científicas, 1985).

CARACOL BAY

A bay on the north coast of **Hispaniola,** east of **Cape Haitien,** enclosed by a barrier reef. **Navidad,** the European settlement which resulted from the wreck of the *Santa María* on the **First Voyage,** is thought to have been just east of this cape at the west end of the bay, south of the opening to the sea at the western end of the barrier reef.

Ref. *AOS*1 I, 393-95, II, 91-96; *AOS*2, 297-305, 428.

CARAVEL

A sailing **ship** developed by the Portuguese for ocean sailing along the coast of Africa, where it was frequently necessary to sail against the wind for long distances. The caravel's most characteristic feature was the triangular **lateen sails,** mounted on two, three, and sometimes four masts. Square rigging could be substituted to take advantage of steady winds in the direction of the destination, as in sailing before the **trade winds** on the voyage to the **West Indies.** CC's 1492 fleet, including the caravels *Niña* and *Pinta*, was rigged this way. The average dimensions of the hull were probably seventy feet (length) and twenty-four feet (beam); the average capacity was fifty to sixty tons. Its small size made it an excellent ship for exploring unknown waters.

Ref. *AOS1* I, xxxvii-xliii, 150-55, II, 55-56, 228-29, 319-23; C. Etayo Elizondo, *Naos y caravelas de los descubrimientos y las naves de Colón* (Pamplona: Aralar, 1971); José María Martínez-Hidalgo, *Columbus' Ships,* ed. Howard I. Chapelle (Barre, MA: Barre Publishers, 1966).

CARDERA

One of the two small (about forty tons), **lateen**-rigged **caravels** that CC took, along with the square-rigged *Niña,* to **Cuba** from **Isabela** in 1494. On this exploration the *Cardera* had Cristóbal Pérez as master (apparently no captain) and a crew of fourteen. It was destroyed in Isabela harbor in the **hurricane** of 1495. From parts of the *Cardera,* the *San Juan,* and another wrecked caravel, CC's shipwrights built a sister ship to the *Niña* named *Santa Cruz,* called *India* by the seamen, the first European ship to be built in the **Indies.**

Ref. *AOS1* II, 55-56, 117-18, 173; *AOS2,* 445, 491; José María Martínez-Hidalgo, "Las naves de los cuatro viajes de Colón al nuevo mundo," *Temi Colombiani* (Genoa: ECIG, 1986), 201-29.

CARIB INDIANS

The natives of the **Lesser Antilles.** Indigenous to Brazil, they emigrated northward to Guiana and the **Antilles,** and conquered the Igneris sometime during the early fifteenth century. They called themselves *Kalinas* (or *Killinagos*). The **Tainos** called them "Caribs"; from this term and its derivitives, the Spanish rendered the word "caribale," or "cannibal." CC's sailors encountered Caribs on the **Second Voyage,** on **Guadeloupe,** around 4 November 1493. Their deserted huts were reported by **Michele de Cuneo** to contain cut-up human torsos ready for cooking. Cuneo claimed that CC's landing party brought some captive **Tainos** back to the fleet, including castrated boys being fattened to eat and girls used to breed babies for food. However, scholars today can find no hard evidence that the Caribs were cannibals.

The idea that Caribs ate people may have stemmed from miscommunication between CC and Taino Indians. Caribs often perpetrated slave raids on the Tainos. When Tainos told CC about the existence of Carib Indians, he thought he heard them say that their people had been eaten by the Caribs, as an explanation for why none of the captives ever returned. But CC's understanding of the **Arawak** language was, by his own admission, quite limited. In fact, the only Carib Indians CC ever directly encountered on St. Croix were actually not Caribs, who modern ethnologists believe did not reside north of Guadeloupe.

At **St. Croix** on about 14 November, the Spaniards had their first recorded fight with natives of the **New World,** perhaps Caribs, whom the Spanish cornered in a **canoe** and captured after a fierce fight in which one Spaniard was killed. After the Spaniards were safely back at their ships, a large number of Indians came and shot futilely at the strangers. Cuneo recorded his capture and rape of a Carib woman at St. Croix, whom CC had allowed him to take as a **slave.** Again, these people were probably not Caribs. The Spanish colonists tended to designate resistant natives as ''Caribs,'' while they often categorized cooperative natives as ''Tainos.''

Ref. *AOS1* II, 68-90, 182-85; *AOS2,* 405-17; *JOD,* 209-28, contains the text of Cuneo's letter; C.J.M.R. Gullick, *Myths of a Minority: The Changing Traditions of the Vincentian Caribs* (Assen: Van Gorcum & Comp., 1985), 25-26, 34; Irving Rouse, ''Origin and Development of the Indians Discovered by Columbus,'' *Proceedings of the First San Salvador Conference: Columbus and His World,* comp. Donald T. Gerace (Ft. Lauderdale: The College Center of the Finger Lakes Bahamian Field Station, 1987), 293-312; Kirkpatrick Sale, *The Conquest of Paradise: Christopher Columbus and the Columbian Legacy* (New York: Knopf, 1990), 129-40, 200-1; Neil L. Whitehead, *Lords of the Tiger Spirit: A History of the Caribs in Colonial Venezuela and Guyana 1498-1820* (Dordrecht/ Providence: Foris Publications, 1988), 9-12, 21-33.

CARRACK

A three-masted vessel whose rapid evolution from the rounded, tub-like Mediterranean sailing ships of the Middle Ages began about 1450. The foremast and mainmast were square-rigged; the aft, or mizzen, mast bore a **lateen** or triangular sail to aid in tacking. The beam was one-third the length of the ship. This ship soon began replacing the **galley** as a cargo vessel. In the **Iberian Peninsula** the carrack was called a nao; CC's flagship on the **First Voyage,** the *Santa María,* was a nao.

Ref. *AOS1* I, xxxvii-xliii, 150-55, II, 55-56, 228-29, 319-23; C. Etayo Elizondo, *Naos y caravelas de los descubrimientos y las naves de Colón* (Pamplona: Aralar, 1971); Carla Rahn Phillips, ''Sizes and Configurations of Spanish Ships in the Age of Discovery,'' *Proceedings of the First San Salvador Conference: Columbus and His World,* comp. Donald T. Gerace (Ft. Lauderdale: The College Center of the Finger Lakes Bahamian Field Station, 1987), 69-98.

CARVAJAL, ALONSO SÁNCHEZ DE (n.d.) The captain of one of the **ships** in the seventeen-vessel fleet that CC commanded on the **Second Voyage.** Carvajal was mayor of the town of Baeza in **Spain,** which had to pay his full salary during the voyage. He was a member of the council appointed by CC to govern **Hispaniola** during his voyage of discovery from 24 April to 29 September 1494. Later, when CC was suspended as **Viceroy of the Indies** and **Ovando** became governor, Carvajal was appointed as CC's factor to ensure that his proper portion of the proceeds from trade and **gold** mining would be paid to him. Partly as a result of Carvajal's faithful discharge of this duty, CC died a wealthy man.

Ref. *AOS*1 II, 228-29; *AOS*2, 512-13, 564-65, 636-39; Juan Gil, "Las cuentas de Cristóbal Colón," *Anuario de Estudios Americanos* (Seville) 41 (1984): 425-511.

CARVAJAL, BERNARDINO DE (ca. 1456-1523)
Priest and Spanish ambassador to Rome who, on 19 June 1493, preached a sermon directed at Pope **Alexander VI,** whose recent **papal bull,** *Inter Caetera* (3 May 1493), dealing with Spanish and Portuguese property in the Atlantic, was not satisfactory to the Spanish crown. Shortly thereafter Alexander issued two more bulls which clarified Spanish privileges in the Atlantic, a revised *Inter Caetera* (antedated as 4 May 1493, actually issued after Carvajal's sermon), and *Eximiae devotionis* (antedated as 3 May 1493, issued in July). The first of these drew the famous **demarcation line** between Spanish and Portuguese claims at thirty-eight degrees West **longitude.** This line was later changed to forty-six degrees thirty minutes West longitude by the Treaty of Tordesillas (1494).

Ref. *AOS*1 II, 24; Edward Gaylord Bourne, "The History and Determination of the Line of Demarcation Established by Pope Alexander VI, between the Spanish and Portuguese Fields of Discovery and Colonization," *Yale Review* 1 (1892): 35-55; H. Van der Linden, "Alexander VI and the Demarcation of the Maritime and Colonial Domains of Spain and Portugal, 1493-1494," *American Historical Review* 22 (1916-17): 1-20.

CASA DE CONTRATACIÓN
An office established in **Seville** for the administration of the conquest and colonization of the **New World,** an activity that began when **Don Juan Rodriguez de Fonseca,** Archbishop of Seville, was put in charge of assembling and outfitting CC's fleet for the **Second Voyage.** The building, later constructed near the Cathedral of Seville for this major Spanish of-

fice, still houses the papers and records accumulated over the centuries while the Spanish empire was active. Under the name "**Archive of the Indies,**" this collection of documents has become the chief resource for historical study of the entire Spanish activity in the New World.

CASAS, BARTOLOMÉ DE LAS
See LAS CASAS, BARTOLOMÉ DE.

CASCAIS
A town in **Portugal,** on the Atlantic, at the mouth of the **Tagus River.** It was the first European town sighted by CC and his crew upon their return from the **First Voyage.**

Ref. *AOS*1 I, 434.

CASENOVE, GUILLAUME DE (n.d.)
The French naval commander whose squadron attacked a Genoese convoy in the Atlantic near **Cape St. Vincent** at the southwest corner of **Portugal** in August 1476. CC is supposed by some scholars to have been aboard a ship in the Genoese convoy, the Flemish *Bechalla*, sunk in the French attack. According to this account, CC grasped a broken oar and with its aid reached the nearby port of **Lagos.** He then proceeded to **Lisbon** where he is known to have been in 1476. Casenove, a vice-admiral of France, bore the nickname "Coullon," which was rendered "Colón" in **Spain;** it seems possible that CC, attracted by

the title of admiral, copied Casenove's nickname when he adopted "Colón" as the Spanish version of his surname. Casenove, known as "Colombo Viejo" or "Columbus Senior," is to be distinguished from **Colombo Junior,** a Greek corsair (Georges Bissipart), also serving the King of France in this period.

Ref. *AOS*1 I, 32, 37, 144; Henry Harrisse, *Les Colombo de France et d'Italie: Fameux marins du xve siècle 1461-1492* (Paris: Librairie Tross, 1874); Alberto Salvagnini, "Colombo e i corsari Colombo suoi conteporanei," *Raccolta di documenti e studi pubblicati dalla R. Commissione colombiana pel quarto centenario della scoperta dell'America,* vol. 2 (Rome: Ministro della Pubblica Istruzione, 1892-96), iii:127-248; Henry Vignaud, *Études critiques sur la vie de Colomb avant ses découvertes* (Paris: Welter, 1905).

CASSAVA BREAD
The bread prepared by the **Taino** natives of the **Bahamas** and **West Indies** from flour derived from the cassava or manioc plant. CC saw this bread in the Bahamas; it can still be found today in both hemispheres. Cassava is the source of tapioca.

Ref. *AOS*1 I and II *passim; AOS*2, 499.

CASTANHEIRA, CONVENTO DE SAN ANTONIO DE

A monastery in **Portugal** where **John II**'s queen, **Leonor,** was sojourning in March of 1493 when CC, forced into Portuguese waters by a **storm** on his return from the **First Voyage,** visited the king at the nearby monastery of **Santa Maria das Virtudes.** At her insistence, CC went to visit Leonor at Castanheira before he left Portugal.

Ref. *AOS*1 I, 442-43; *AOS*2, 346-48.

CASTANHEIRA, JOÃO DE (n.d.)

The captain of **Santa Maria Island** in the **Azores,** where CC stopped while returning to **Spain** on the **First Voyage.** When CC sent part of his crew ashore to make votive prayers at a chapel, Castanheira, who enforced **John II**'s jealous resentment of non-Portuguese voyages in the Atlantic, arrested and held them. Later, he tried to capture CC and the rest of his crew but was outwitted by CC, who recovered his men by threatening to sail on to Spain and send forces to devastate the islands.

Ref. *AOS*1 I, 426-30; *AOS*2, 332-35.

CASTILE

The former kingdom in the **Iberian Peninsula** extending from the Bay of Biscay south to the Atlantic Ocean and the Mediterranean Sea, bounded on the west by **Portugal,** on the southeast by **Granada,** and on the east by **Aragón.** When CC arrived in 1485, Castile, under Queen **Isabel I,** had recently been combined with the kingdom of Aragón, under King **Ferdinand V,** to form the kingdom of **Spain.** As the larger region, Castile dominated the new kingdom; and as the western region with natural interests in the Atlantic, it dominated the pioneering and conquest of the **New World.** Castilian was the dominant literary and diplomatic language of the Iberian Peninsula and became the standard language of Spain.

Ref. R.B. Merriman, *The Rise of the Spanish Empire in the Old World and the New,* vol. 1 (New York: Macmillan, 1936).

CASTILLA

A **caravel** on CC's **Third Voyage.** *See* SHIPS, CC'S.

CAT ISLAND

An island in the **Bahamas** northwest of Watlings that, along with Watlings, **Grand Turk, Samana Cay,** and others, has been proposed as the site of CC's 1492 **landfall.** *See* SAN SALVADOR.

Ref. John Parker, "The Columbus Landfall Problem: A Historical Perspective," eds. Louis De Vorsey and John Parker, *In the Wake of Columbus: Islands and Controversy* (Detroit: Wayne State University Press, 1985), 1-28.

CATHOLIC MONARCHS

Ferdinand and **Isabel,** joint monarchs of **Spain,** reigned 1479-1504. The name "Catholic" was commonly used in CC's day to indicate their commitment to the Roman Catholic Church and to their goal of making the entire population of their combined monarchies Roman Catholic. The great achievement of the early part of their reign was the defeat of the Moorish kingdom of **Granada,** whose surrender in 1492 ended the passionate effort of the Hispanic Christian community over a period of 700 years to reclaim the peninsula. Despite the popular notion that the Catholic monarchs, and especially Ferdinand, were unreasonable in making CC wait seven years (1485-92) before adopting and funding his **Enterprise of the Indies,** the determining factor here was undoubtedly the desire to end the Moorish war before undertaking anything else. After the Moorish surrender on 2 January 1492, the Enterprise was reconsidered. In spite of further strong disagreements with CC (mainly over his demands for personal advancement), the monarchs accepted the proposal on surprisingly generous terms as registered in the **Capitulations of 1492;** in barely three months from the date of this agreement, CC's fleet was assembled, outfitted, and manned in time to sail for the **Indies** on 3 August, only seven months almost to the day after the fall of Granada.

The monarchs attempted with commendable integrity to live up to the concessions made to CC in the Capitulations. They received him at **Barcelona** when he returned from the **First Voyage** and showered him with kudos, promptly commissioning a large fleet for the **Second Voyage.** After they were forced to act against CC's alleged incompetence in **Hispaniola,** empowering **Francisco de Bobadilla** to remove him from office, the monarchs upheld as much of the agreement as they could, requiring Bobadilla to make restitution to CC for the damages done to his personal estate in the course of his removal from office. Even after Isabel's death, Ferdinand was sufficiently committed to the agreement with CC to appoint CC's heir, **Diego,** as second **Viceroy of the Indies** and second **Admiral of the Oceans.** Moreover, he did not block the lawsuit (**Los Pleitos**) that Diego and **Ferdinand Columbus** brought against the crown in 1509 to seek full enforcement of the terms of the Capitulations. The suit continued over many years but was finally resolved favorably for CC's heirs.

Ref. R.B. Merriman, *The Rise of the Spanish Empire in the Old World and the New,* vol. 1 (New York: Macmillan, 1936).

CENTURIONE

A Genoese banking and merchant family with whom CC had long-term ties and for whom he was a factor in an attempt to purchase sugar in **Madeira** in 1478. In his will, CC left bequests to members of the Centurione family and two closely-related Genoese commercial families, the **Spinola** and **di Negro** families. When CC went to **Chios,** he was probably working for one of these three families. *See* FUNCHAL.

Ref. *AOS*1 I, 30-52, II, 227.

CHACACHACARE ISLAND

The modern name of the island that CC called "El Caracol," the westernmost of three islands lying across the northern egress of the **Gulf of París,** at the mouth of the **Orinoco** River, between **Trinidad** and the París Peninsula in **Venezuela.** The three islands separate the four northern mouths of the gulf, the **Bocas del Dragon,** so named by CC when he discovered the area in August 1498 while en route to **Hispaniola** during the **Third Voyage.**

Ref. *AOS*1 II, 259, 275; *AOS*2, 538, 549.

CHACHU (d. ca. 1492)

A boatswain of the *Santa María* on the **First Voyage.** He was one of the sailors who chose to remain at the makeshift fort **Navidad** when CC was forced to leave part of his crew in **Haiti** after the wreck of the *Santa María* in December 1492.

Ref. *AOS*1 I, 188-90, 394; *AOS*2, 538, 549.

CHANCA, DIEGO ALVAREZ (n.d.)

A physician of **Seville** who sailed on the **Second Voyage** and left a detailed account of it in the "Letter of Dr. Diego Alvarez Chanca." He was extremely attentive to the sailors and colonists during the difficult days of sickness after the fleet arrived in **Hispaniola** and the town of **Isabela** was founded.

Ref. *AOS*1 II, 56, 65-101 *passim,* 209; *AOS*2, 396-435; Cecil Jane, ed. and trans., *Select Documents Illustrating the Four Voyages of Columbus,* vol. 1, ser. 2, no. 65 (London: Hakluyt Society Publications, 1930), the text of a letter.

CHARLES VIII (1470-1498)

King of France (1483-1498). During his minority his sister **Anne of Beaujeu** served as regent. She showed hospitality to CC's brother **Bartholomew Columbus** when he visited the court to seek support for CC's **Enterprise of the Indies.** Bartholomew was still at the French court in August 1492 when CC sailed on the **First Voyage.**

Ref. *AOS*1 II, 193-204 *passim.*

CHERSONESE, GOLDEN

See GOLDEN CHERSONESE.

CHIOS

A Greek island in the Aegean Sea near Turkey where the Genoese maintained a trading colony in the fifteenth century. CC reported in the *Journal* on 12 November and 10 December 1492, and in the **Letter to Santangel** of 4 March 1493, that he had seen **mastic** gathered from the lentisk tree in Chios. He probably visited Chios on one of the Genoese expeditions to the island in 1474 and 1475, which included people from CC's Genoese suburb **Savona** on ships owned by the **Spinola** and **di Negro** families, with whom CC was associated much of his life.

> Ref. *AOS1* I, 30-31; *AOS2*, 22-23, 259; Laura Balletto, ''Chio nel tempo di Cristoforo Colombo,'' *Atti del III Convegno Internazionale di Studi Colombiani 1977* (Genoa: Civico Istituto Colombiano, 1979), 175-98.

CHIRIQUI LAGOON
A lagoon in **Costa Rica** emptying into the Caribbean, one of several that CC felt might turn out to be the strait to the Indian Ocean. CC visited here from 5 to 16 October 1502 on the **Fourth Voyage** and named the lagoon ''Alburema Bay.''

> Ref. *AOS2*, 605-7.

CIBAO
An Indian name for central **Hispaniola** which CC took to mean ''Cipangu'' or **Japan**. On the **First Voyage**, CC heard that there were **gold** mines in the area, news that motivated him to found the Spanish colony of **Isabela.**

> Ref. *AOS1* I, 383-97, II, 102-12, map 2.

CIGUAYO INDIANS
A tribe of **Indians** living near Samaná Bay in northern **Hispaniola** with whom CC's crew had a brief skirmish on 13 January 1493.

> Ref. *AOS1* I, 399-404; *AOS2*, 311-13, 422, 564.

CIUDAD TRUJILLO
A twentieth-century name for **Santo Domingo.**

COAT OF ARMS
See HERALDRY.

COLINA
A nao that was one of the seventeen **ships** in CC's fleet on the **Second Voyage.**

> Ref. *AOS1* II, 55; Alicia Bache Gould, ''Nueva lista documentada de los tripulantes de Colón en 1492,'' *Boletin de la real Academia della Historia* (Madrid) 85 (1924): 353-79.

COLOMA, JUAN DE (n.d.)
The man who represented the Spanish sovereigns in the negotiations with CC that led to the signing of the **Capitulations of 1492.**

> Ref. *AOS1* I, 138, II, 416.

COLOMBINA, BIBLIOTECA
See BIBLIOTECA COLOMBINA.

COLOMBO, BARTOLOMEO
CC's brother. See COLUMBUS, BARTHOLOMEW.

COLOMBO, CRISTOFORO

The Italian rendering of CC's name.

COLOMBO, DIEGO (GIACOMO COLOMBO) (ca. 1468-ca. 1515)

CC's youngest sibling, baptized Giacomo Colombo (*Diego* is the Spanish equivalent of Giacomo). He accompanied CC on the **Second Voyage** and was appointed head of the governing council formed by CC when he left **Hispaniola** temporarily in 1494 to explore the south coast of **Cuba.** Diego was a poor administrator and was sent back to **Spain** as a prisoner with CC by the chief justice and royal commissioner **Francisco de Bobadilla** to stand trial with CC for misgovernment. The charges were dropped in Spain. Later Diego took up a religious vocation; CC hoped to get him a bishopric, but nothing came of this.

> Ref. *AOS*1 I, 13-22, II, 57-58, 310-11; *AOS*2, 482-87, 569-71.

COLOMBO, DOMENICO

CC's father. See COLOMBO FAMILY OF GENOA.

COLOMBO, GIACOMO

CC's brother. *See* COLOMBO, DIEGO.

COLOMBO, GIOVANNI (GIANNETTO) (b. ca. 1446)

A first cousin of CC. His agreement with his brothers, Mateus and Amigetus, in **Genoa** to go to **Spain,** seek out CC, and request employment, is a chief documentary proof of CC's Genoese origin. CC gave him the command of a **caravel** in the **Third Voyage.**

> Ref. *AOS*1 I, 16-17, II, 229, 236, 296, 412; *AOS*2, 14, 513, 518, 661.

COLOMBO FAMILY OF GENOA

Founded by CC's grandfather, **Giovanni Colombo,** a weaver who moved to **Quinto,** a suburb east of **Genoa** from **Moconesi,** northeast of Genoa. His son Domenico, CC's father, a master weaver, married Susanna Fontanarossa. Domenico, active politically, was moderately prosperous when his party was in power. His children by Susanna included CC, Bartolomeo (**Bartholomew Colombo**), and Giacomo (**Diego Colombo**), as well as Giovanni Pellegrino, who died young, and a daughter, Bianchinetta. During CC's childhood, the family lived in a house in Genoa near the Porto Soprano. When CC was in his teens, Domenico moved the family to the nearby town of **Savona.**

> Ref. *AOS*1 I, 12-17; City of Genoa, *Christopher Columbus: Documents and Proofs of His Genoese Origin* (Genoa: Istituto d'Arti Grafiche, 1931); P.E. Taviani, *La Genovesità di Colombo* (Genoa: ECIG, 1987).

COLOMBO JUNIOR (BISSIPART) (n.d.)

Nickname of a Greek corsair named Georges Bissipart in the service of King Louis XI of France. **Ferdinand Columbus,** in compiling his biography of CC, the *Historie*, reported that CC was fighting on the side of the corsairs when shipwrecked during a sea fight between corsairs and merchant vessels. Ferdinand thought that the corsair commanding in this fight was Colombo Junior, who attacked some Venetian **galleys** in 1485; Ferdinand even claimed kinship with this corsair. All this is simply fiction, but a similar fight occurred between a Genoese convoy and French corsairs led by **Guillaume de Casenove,** also nicknamed "Coullon," and referred to as "Colombo Senior" to distinguish him from Bissipart. Some scholars think CC was on a Genoese ship that was sunk in this fight off **Cape St. Vincent** in August 1476, and that he initially entered **Portugal** by swimming ashore near **Lagos** after the sinking.

Ref. *AOS*1 I, 36-37; Henry Harrisse, *Les Colombo de France et d'Italie: Fameux marins du xve siècle 1461-1492* (Paris: Librairie Tross, 1874); Alberto Salvagnini, "Colombo e i corsari Colombo suoi conteporanei," *Raccolta di documenti e studi pubblicati dalla R. Commissione colombiana pel quarto centenario della scoperta dell'America,* vol. 1 (Rome: Ministro della Pubblica Istruzione, 1892-96), 127-248; Henry Vignaud, *Études critiques sur la vie de Colomb avant ses découvertes* (Paris: Welter, 1905).

COLÓN, CRISTÓBAL
The Spanish rendering of CC's name.

COLÓN, DIEGO
CC's son. *See* **COLUMBUS, DIEGO.**

COLÓN, DIEGO (INDIAN) (n.d.)
One of the **Taino Indians** whom CC took captive in the **Bahamas,** perhaps on **Guanahani,** and who soon became so proficient in Spanish that CC made him his chief interpreter in dealing with the West Indians. He was baptized Diego Colón in **Barcelona** in 1493 with the Spanish monarchs and their son **Prince Don Juan** as godparents. Diego returned to **Hispaniola** with CC on the **Second Voyage** and then was sent back to **Spain** with **Antonio de Torres** in 1495 to counter the bad publicity deriving from **Fray Bernal Buil** and other persons who had returned in 1494 from Hispaniola.

Ref. *AOS*1 I, 337-38, II, 14, 92, 133-39; *AOS*2, 256-57, 275, 345, 360, 458, 464.

COLÓN, FERNANDO
CC's son. *See* **COLUMBUS, FERDINAND.**

COLÓN, LUIS (ca. 1521-1572)
CC's grandson, the third **Admiral of the Ocean** and **Viceroy of the Indies,** who succeeded his father Don **Diego Columbus** upon the latter's death in 1526. Don Luis was an irresponsible and incompetent young man. While still a minor under the judicious eye of his mother, **María Colón**

y **Toledo,** he was eased out of the post of viceroy and the other titles and privileges ceded to CC in the **Capitulations of 1492,** in exchange for the Duchy of **Veragua.** Don Luis, a womanizer and polygamist, outrageously dissipated the Colón estate, including many of the most important books in his Uncle **Ferdinand Columbus's** great library, thus seriously hindering Columbus scholarship.

Ref. *AOS*1 I, 69, II, 360, 416, 425; Luis Arranz Márquez, *Don Diego Colón, Almirante, Virrey y Gobernador de las Indias,* vol. 1 (Madrid: Consejo Superior de Investigaciones Científicas, 1982).

COLÓN Y TOLEDO, MARÍA DE (n.d.)
Wife of **Diego Columbus,** *virreina* (wife of the viceroy) of the Indies, and mother of **Luis Colón,** third admiral of the Indies. Her position as a cousin of King **Ferdinand** assured Diego's succession to CC's title and position as admiral and **Viceroy of the Indies.** As virreina and guardian of Don Luis Colón during his nonage, she wisely traded CC's privilege under the **Capitulations of 1492** for the Duchy of **Veragua.** CC's descendant still holds the title "Duke of Veragua."

Ref. *AOS*1 I, 113, II, 350, 416; *AOS*2, 85, 609, 665; Luis Arranz Márquez, "La noblesa colombina y sus relaciones con la Castellana," *Revista de Indias* (Madrid) 35 (1975): 83-122; John Boyd

Thacher, *Christopher Columbus: His Life, His Works, His Remains,* 3 vols. (New York: Putnam, 1903-4), 3: 617-41.

COLUMBUS, BARTHOLOMEW (BARTOLOMEO COLOMBO) (ca. 1461-1514)
A younger brother of CC, possibly by as much as ten years, since CC was born in 1451 and Bartholomew testified in 1512 that he was "fifty or older." Bartholomew was born in **Genoa;** he might have been in **Lisbon** as early as 1476 when CC arrived. Presumably, Bartholomew went to sea early, like CC and other Genoese, and may have been apprenticed to a mapmaker, since he seems to have supported himself at this trade from time to time. He was sent by CC at some time in the late 1480s to present the **Enterprise of the Indies** to **Henry VII** of **England;** failing there, he proceeded to the court of **Charles VIII** of France, where he attached himself to the household of the king's sister **Anne de Beaujeu,** regent during the minority of the king, with the purpose of selling the Enterprise to France. While he was still there in 1493, he was summoned by King Charles to receive the news of CC's discovery of the **Indies.**

Going to **Spain,** Bartholomew took passage to **Hispaniola,** where CC promptly made him his second in command, giving him the title of **adelantado,** which was later confirmed by the crown. When CC returned to Spain in 1496 to defend himself against the accusations of former colonists, he left Bartholomew in charge; it was Bartholomew who established the original settlement of **Santo Domingo,** the oldest surviving Spanish settlement in the Western Hemisphere. Later, Bartholomew had to deal with the rebellion of disaffected colonists under **Roldán,** who continued to plague the Columbus brothers until the royal commissioner and chief justice **Francisco de Bobadilla** arrived and sent the three brothers—CC, Bartholomew, and **Diego Colombo**—home in chains to face charges of maladministration; the charges were dropped by the crown when CC appeared before the Spanish sovereigns.

Bartholomew accompanied CC on the **Fourth Voyage** and played a key role in CC's explorations throughout. Afterward he worked in the interests of CC in Spain until the latter's death. Later he went to Rome to solicit (unsuccessfully) the Pope's sponsorship of a project for Spanish settlement of the Panamanian area of **Veragua.** In 1509 he returned to Hispaniola with his nephew **Diego Columbus,** the new viceroy, and continued to bear the title of adelantado. His movements after that time are not entirely clear. He testified in 1512 in Spain in Diego's suit against the crown, and died, perhaps in the **Indies,** about 1514. He was interred in 1514 in the Carthusian monastery of **Las Cuevas** in **Seville** where CC was buried. When CC's remains were transferred to the Cathedral of Santo Domingo, around 1541, in accordance with Diego's wishes, Bartholomew's body presumably stayed at Las Cuevas.

Ref. *AOS*2, 12-14, 35-36, 90-91, 364, 481-82, 484-94, 497-98, 560-71, 585, 591, 599, 663, 665, 668-69; Aldo Albonico, "Bartolomeo Colombo, adelantado mayor de las Indias," eds. A. Boscolo and B. Torres, *La presenza italiana in Andalusia nel basso medioevo. Atti del II Colloquio Italiano-Spagnolo, Roma, 25-27 maggio 1984* (Bologna: Cappelli, 1986), 51-70.

COLUMBUS, DIEGO (DIEGO COLÓN) (ca. 1480-1526)

CC's son by **Felipa Perestrello e Moniz,** the Portuguese woman of prominent family whom CC married sometime between 1477 and 1480. CC took Diego to **Spain** in 1485 to seek support for his **Enterprise of the Indies** from the Spanish monarchs and, presumably, left him with the friars for schooling at **La Rábida** near **Palos** while he continued his suit with the Spanish court during the years 1485 to 1491. When CC returned from discovering the **West Indies,** the monarchs accorded to Diego and his half-brother **Ferdinand** positions as pages at court where they were educated as courtiers. Diego married **María Colón y Toledo,** daughter of a prominent Spanish noble and cousin of King **Ferdinand.** She became the *virreina* (wife of the viceroy) of the Indies and mother of **Luis Colón.** After CC's death Diego received the inherited titles of admiral and **Viceroy of the Indies** and ruled as viceroy in his capital in **Santo Domingo** until his death in 1526.

Many scholars think that the body entombed as Christopher Columbus in the cathedral at **Seville** is actually that of Diego, exhumed mistakenly (instead of Christopher's) from its tomb in the cathedral at Santo Domingo and transferred to Havana when the Spanish ceded Santo Domingo to the French in the eighteenth century. The remains were moved to Seville for burial in the cathedral when **Cuba** became independent of Spain at the end of the Spanish-American war in 1898.

Don Diego initiated a long suit that the heirs of CC conducted against the Spanish crown to collect the privileges detailed in the **Capitulations of 1492.** The records of this suit, known as **Los Pleitos,** are a chief documentary source of information on CC.

Ref. *AOS*1 I, 112-13, II, 229, 411-20; *AOS*2, 39-40, 79, 84-85, 328, 577, 660-69; T.S. Floyd, *The Columbian Dynasty in the Caribbean, 1492-1527* (Albuquerque: University of New Mexico Press, 1973); Luis Arranz Márquez, "La noblesa colombina y sus relaciones con la Castellana," *Revista de Indias* (Madrid) 35 (1975): 83-122; John Boyd Thacher, *Christopher Columbus: His Life, His Works, His Remains,* 3 vols. (New York: Putnam, 1903-4), 3: 617-41.

COLUMBUS, DONA FELIPA PERESTRELLO E MONIZ
See **PERESTRELLO E MONIZ, FELIPA, MONIZ FAMILY** and **PERESTRELLO FAMILY.**

COLUMBUS, FERDINAND (FERNANDO COLÓN) (1488-1539)
CC's illegitimate son by **Beatriz Enríquez de Harana,** born in **Córdova** in August 1488. After CC's successful return from the **First Voyage** in 1493, Ferdinand was legitimatized and he and CC's older son, **Diego Columbus,** were trained as courtiers at the Spanish court, beginning as pages. Ferdinand, who accompanied CC on the **Fourth Voyage,** wrote a biography of his father, usually known as the *Historie*, which has survived only in an Italian translation published in 1571. Ferdinand was a good friend of **Bartholomew de Las Casas,** who used Ferdinand's biography in writing the biography of CC that constitutes part of his great *Historia de las Indias.* Ferdinand became not only a widely-acquainted scholar who knew Erasmus, but one of the greatest book collectors of his time, assembling a library of 4231 volumes that included a number of books owned

and annotated by CC. These books constitute the core of the Columbus Library, the **Biblioteca Colombina,** at the Cathedral of **Seville,** still a significant depository of basic primary documents in spite of the progressive deterioration of the library under CC's prodigal grandson **Luis Colón** and the not always attentive ecclesiastical custodians at the cathedral. Ferdinand is generally thought to have been the most urbane and cordial member of CC's immediate family.

Ref. *AOS*1 I, 68-70, II, 409-20 *passim; AOS*2, 49-50; Emiliano Jos, *Investigaciones sobre la vida y obras iniciales de don Fernando Colón* (Seville: Escuela de Estudios Hispano-Americanos, 1945); Juan Manzano Manzano, *La legitimación de Hernando Colón* (Seville: University of Seville, 1960); Antonio Rumeu de Armas, *Hernando Colón, historiador del descubrimiento de América* (Madrid: Instituto de Cultura Hispánica, 1973); John Boyd Thacher, *Christopher Columbus: His Life, His Works, His Remains,* 3 vols. (New York: Putnam, 1903-4), 3: 617-41.

COMPASS DECLINATION

The angle between the bearing of magnetic north and true north at any particular point on the globe. Because this angle changes as one circles the earth, compass declination in Europe differs from compass declination in the **West Indies.** In Europe, declination is easterly; in the Carib-

bean, westerly. An easterly declination had been observed in Europe in medieval times, but CC was probably the first to observe the change that occurs in crossing the Atlantic.

Besides the discrepancy between the bearing of true north and magnetic north, the angle between the bearing of magnetic north and the bearing of the North Star changes from hour to hour because the eccentric shape and rotation of the earth causes the star to seem to describe a circle of a degree or more in radius around the earth's pole. In 1492, when the radius of this circle was much larger than one degree, there was a noticeable wandering of the bearing of the North Star in a twelve-hour period, a fact that caused consternation and some fear in Columbus's crew.

Ref. *AOS*1 I, 246-47, 270-71; *AOS*2, 189-90, 203; Alberto Magnaghi, ''Incertezze e contrasti delle fonte tradizionali sulle osservazioni attribuite a Colombo intorno ai fenomeni della declinazione magnetica,'' *Bollettino Società Geografica Italiana* (Rome) 10, ser. 6 (1933): 595-641; A. Crichton Mitchell, ''The Discovery of the Magnetic Declination,'' *Terrestrial Magnetism and Atmospheric Electricity* 42 (1937): 241-80.

CONCEPCIÓN DE LA VEGA

The fortress in **Hispaniola** on the trail between **Isabela** and **Santo Domingo** where, in 1498, the adelantado, **Bartholomew Columbus,** temporarily held off the rebel leader **Roldán** while CC was absent from Hispaniola between the **Second** and **Third Voyages.**

Ref. *AOS1* II, 296-98.

CONTRATACIÓN, CASA DE
See CASA DE CONTRATACIÓN.

CONVERSO

The Spanish word designating a person who has been converted to the Christian religion; in CC's time, especially a converted **Jew** or **Moslem.** Converts and their descendants are sometimes referred to as "the Converso community," though the distinction between former Jews and former Moslems is usually maintained. In attempts to assimilate and avoid persecution some Jews opted to convert to Roman Catholicism, especially by the end of the fourteenth century and through the fifteenth century in **Spain.**

Ref. Lee Anne Durham Seminario, *The History of the Blacks, the Jews and the Moors in Spain* (Madrid: Playor, S.A., 1975).

CORDERA

One of **CC's ships** in the **Third Voyage.** This ship remained with the main fleet which sailed from the **Canary Islands** to the **Cape Verde Islands,** and from there to **Trinidad** and South **America.**

Ref. *AOS1* II, 229, 237, 268, 280, 298; *AOS2*, 83-85, 353, 358.

CÓRDOVA

A city on the **Guadalquivir River** in Andalusia, seat of the ancient Caliphate of the **Moors.** Córdova was the temporary capital of King **Ferdinand** and Queen **Isabel** during the war with **Granada.** CC lived in Córdova during much of the time that a royal commission appointed by the Spanish sovereigns was evaluating his **Enterprise of the Indies.** He probably worked as a bookseller and mapmaker during this time. It was here that he met **Beatriz Enríquez de Harana,** who gave birth to his illegitimate son, **Ferdinand Columbus,** in August 1488.

Ref. *AOS1* I, 67, 111-13, 422, II, 6, 11, 54; *AOS2*, 83-85, 353, 358.

CORN
See MAIZE.

CORONEL, PEDRO FERNÁNDEZ DE (n.d.)

Ship commander on CC's **Second Voyage,** and also a member of the governing council, headed by **Diego Colombo,** that CC set up to govern **Hispaniola** during the period when he was absent exploring the south coast of **Cuba.** During the **Third Voyage,** Coronel's ship was part of the advance squadron of CC's fleet which sailed directly to Hispaniola instead of heading for **Trinidad** as did the main fleet. Because the squadron missed **Santo Domingo** and landed too far west in Hispaniola, it arrived in the capital after the main fleet. While in western Hispaniola, he was instrumental in confirming **Bartholomew Columbus's** authority vis-à-vis the **Roldán** rebels by presenting the royal order confirming Bartholomew as **adelantado.**

Ref. *AOS*1 II, 56, 115, 228, 296; *AOS*2, 396, 444, 512, 564.

CORREA DA CUNHA, PEDRO (n.d.)

A man to whom **Dona Isabel Moniz e Perestrello,** mother-in-law of CC, sold her interest in the captaincy of the island of **Porto Santo** in the **Madeiras** after the death of her husband, Don Bartholomew Perestrello. Later, this arrangement was annulled and Isabel's son Bartholomew succeeded as captain of Porto Santo, where Columbus and his wife, Felipa, probably lived for a time after their marriage, from 1477 to 1479.

Ref. *AOS*1 I, 50, 82.

CORVO

The westernmost of the **Azores Islands,** discovered by **Diogo de Teive** in 1452. CC is said to have visited Corvo in Portuguese ships, and to have seen there a rock resembling a horseman pointing west. He presumably regarded this as a confirmation of his ambitions.

Ref. *AOS*1 I, 41, 79-80.

COSA, JUAN DE LA

See LA COSA, JUAN DE.

COSTA DE LAS OREJAS

The northern Caribbean coast of **Honduras,** site of CC's first **landfall** in Central **America,** 14 August 1502, during the **Fourth Voyage.** CC called it the "Coast of the Ears" because of the natives' practice of drilling large holes in their ears to insert ornaments.

Ref. *AOS*1 II, 336.

COSTA RICA

A Central American country whose Caribbean coast CC discovered during the **Fourth Voyage** sometime between 17 and 24 September 1503.

Ref. *AOS*1 II, 339-42; Academia de Geografía e Historia de Costa Rica, *Colección de documentos para la historia de Costa Rica relativos al cuarto y último viaje de Cristóbal Colón* (San José, Costa Rica: Atenea, 1952), with prologue and introduction by Jorge A. Lines.

COTTON

This plant, though cultivated in Egypt, China, and India before the Christian era, was also grown by the **Indian** natives of the Caribbean before CC arrived; it was the chief raw material for fabrics used by the Indians, notably the coarse fabric of which **hammocks** were made.

Ref. *AOS*2, 242, 245; Kirkpatrick Sale, *The Conquest of Paradise: Christopher Columbus and the Columbian Legacy* (New York: Knopf, 1990), 98.

COULLON
See CASENOVE, GUILLAUME DE.

CREDENCE, LETTER OF

One of the documents given to CC as part of his diplomatic portfolio when he set out on the **First Voyage.** It confirmed CC as the Spanish sovereigns' representative, and included a cordial greeting. It was copied in triplicate and addressed to "the most serene prince," presumably to be presented to the rulers of China or **Japan,** or whatever potentates CC might encounter. A blank was left for insertion of the appropriate name.

Ref. *AOS1* I, 141; *AOS2*, 107; *JOD,* 30-31.

CRIMINALS AS COLONISTS

In establishing the orders for the **Third Voyage,** the Spanish sovereigns, on 15 June 1497, declared that all criminals, except those convicted of the most severe crimes like heresy and first-degree murder, could receive pardon by going to **Hispaniola** with CC and remaining as colonists for a specified length of time (depending on the seriousness of the crime). A law of the same date authorized judges to banish certain criminals to hard labor in the **Indies.** This was presumably the precedent for later decisions to deport European criminals to Georgia (British America) and Australia.

Ref. *AOS1* II, 226.

CRIMINALS IN CC'S CREW

One of the most persistent myths about CC is that his crews on the **First Voyage** consisted largely of criminals cleared from Spanish jails for the purpose. Actually the crews consisted mostly of skilled and responsible seamen from the vicinity of **Palos,** recruited mainly by **Martín Alonso Pinzón.** Four crew members, however, **Bartolomé de Torres,** Alonso Clavijo, Juan de Moguer, and Pedro Yzquierdo, were under sentence of death *in absentia* when they signed up. Torres was under sentence for killing a man; the others, for helping him escape. They gave no trouble on the voyage and, when they returned, successfully avoided further prosecution by citing the royal order that had suspended civil and criminal processes against those who signed up for the crews.

Ref. *AOS1* I, 184; Alicia Bache Gould, "Nuevos datos sobre Colón y otros descubridores: Datos nuevos sobre el primer viaje de Colón," *Boletin de al Real Academia de la Historia* (Madrid) 76 (1920): 201-14.

CROOKED ISLAND AND CROOKED ISLAND PASSAGE

The island and sea passage in the **Bahama Islands** about 150 miles south of **San Salvador Island.** Morison traces CC's route through the Bahamas, in the days following the 12 October **landfall,** to Crooked Island, identifying it as CC's **Isabela Island,** and through the passage between Crooked Island and **Long Island,** which Morison identifies as CC's **Fernandina.** Other scholars frequently disagree with this analysis.

Ref. *AOS1* I, 320-29; Joseph Judge, "Where Columbus Found the New World," *National Geographic* 170 (November 1986): 566-99; Robert H. Power, "The Discovery of Columbus' Island Passage to Cuba, 12-27 October 1492," Louis De Vorsey and John Parker, eds. *In the Wake of Columbus: Islands and Controversy* (Detroit: Wayne State University Press, 1985), 151-72.

CRUSADES
See **JERUSALEM.**

CRUZ, CAPE
A cape at the southeast corner of **Cuba** named by CC on 3 May 1494 during the **Fourth Voyage.** The name has survived to modern times.

Ref. *AOS1* II, 122-23.

CUBA
The largest island in the **West Indies.** CC discovered the island on 27 October 1492, naming it Juana. He explored the shore and some inland of the area now known as **Oriente Province** and discovered **tobacco** and barkless dogs, but no minerals or settlements larger than villages. CC was convinced that Cuba was attached to the Asiatic mainland and, on the

Second Voyage, after exploring the south coast almost to the western extremity, concluded he was not exploring an island. In an extraordinary ritual of uncertainty, he required the entire crew to swear that Cuba was part of the Asiatic mainland. Cuba was circumnavigated by Sebastian de Ocampo in 1509, but the **Juan de La Cosa** map, dated 1500, suggests that Cuba was known to be an island well before Ocampo's voyage.

Ref. *AOS1* II, 433; Roberto Barreiro Meiro, "Algo sobre la carta de Juan de la Cosa," *Rev Gen Marina* (Madrid) 183 (1972): 3-8; José Manuel Pérez Cabrera, *En Tomo al Bojeo de Cuba* (Havana, 1941).

CUEVAS, LAS
The Carthusian monastery across from the **Guadalquivir River** from **Seville,** where CC's close friend **Fray Gaspar Gorricio** was living at the time CC was returned in chains from **Hispaniola.** CC's body was buried here after being removed from its initial burial site in **Valladolid,** prior to being taken to Hispaniola for burial in the cathedral at **Santo Domingo.**

Ref. *AOS2*, 577-78; C. Fernández Duro, "Noticias di la muerte de d. Cristóbal Colón y del lugar de enterramiento en Valladolid," *Boletin de la Real Academia de la Historia* (Madrid) 24 (1894): 44-46; E. Tejera, "Acta de la entrega y deposito del cuerpo de D. Cristóbal Colón en el Monasterio de Santa María de las Cuevas de Sevilla,'' *Clio* (Santo Domingo, July-August 1933): 94-96; John Boyd Thacher, *Christopher Columbus: His Life, His Work, His Remains,* 3 vols. (New York: Putnam, 1903-4), 3: 491, 503, 507, 512-13, 514-21, 603-13.

CUNA CUNA INDIANS

Also known by the Spanish as "San Blas" Indians. Whether they belonged to a subculture of **Tainos, Caribs,** or Guanahatabeys (the three dominant ethnic groups in the Caribbean area explored by CC) was not specified. CC and his men may have encountered Cuna Cuna Indians during the **Fourth Voyage** at Porto Bello and Retrete (modern-day **Panama**). In 1503 Pocorosa was a Cuna Cuna **cacique,** according to CC.

Ref. *AOS2,* 613-17, 635.

CUNEO, MICHELE DE (n.d.)

A native of **Savona** near **Genoa,** of a noble family, he may have been a boyhood friend of CC. He accompanied CC on the **Second Voyage** and, after his return, sent a letter dated 28 October 1495 to a fellow citizen, Hieronymo Annari, describing the voyage. This letter is one of the most extensive accounts of the Second Voyage and certainly the most colorful. It describes the journey from **Cádiz** to **Hispaniola, Hojeda**'s first expedition to explore the interior of Hispaniola, and CC's voyage of discovery along the southern coast of **Cuba** to **Jamaica.** The letter includes numerous interesting observations on the flora, fauna, and human inhabitants of the **West Indies.**

Ref. *AOS1* II, 150-51; *JOD,* 209-28, text of the letter, with elaborate annotations and information about Cuneo himself.

CUNEO, SEBASTIANO (n.d.)

The father of **Michele de Cuneo,** from whom CC's father, **Domenico Colombo,** bought a house near **Savona** in 1494. In January 1501, Cuneo was suing Domenico's heirs for payment of the money that Domenico still owed when he died; court testimony reveals that CC and his immediate family had moved to **Spain.**

Ref. *AOS1* I, 17; Henry Harrisse, *Christopher Columbus and the Bank of St. George* (New York: privately published, 1888).

D

D'AILLY, PIERRE (1350-ca. 1420)
The cardinal of Cambrai ca. 1410, who wrote a geography of the world that CC studied and annotated extensively. *See IMAGO MUNDI.*

D'ANJOU, RENÉ
See **RENÉ D'ANJOU.**

DAY, JOHN (n.d.)
An English wine and woolen merchant, also known as Hugh Say, who was at **Bristol** in 1492/93. Later he lived in **Seville** and perhaps knew CC there. In 1497 he wrote a letter to the admiral of **Castile,** perhaps CC, detailing the **John Cabot** voyage to **Newfoundland;** the letter indicated that he was sending a copy of *The Book of Ser Marco Polo* to the addressee. Some scholars contend that this was the copy of the book owned and annotated by CC and now in the **Biblioteca Colombina** in Seville. If so, this would show that CC did not write his **postils** to **Marco Polo** prior to his **First Voyage,** and strongly suggests that his postils generally do not record his developing thought about the **Enterprise of the Indies** but rather, as Juan Gils argues, record one aspect of his vexed attempt to counter the resentment and accusations to which he was subject as his position in **Spain** grew progressively more difficult in the mid- and late-1490s.

Ref. *EDA1* 205-9, including an English translation of the Day letter; Juan Gil, ed. and trans., *El libro de Marco Polo anotado por Cristóbal Colón. El libro de Marco Polo: version de Rodrigo de Santiella* (Madrid: Alianza, 1987), i-lxix; David B. Quinn, "John Day and Columbus," *Geographical Journal* (London) 133 (1967): 205-9; Consuelo Varela, "John Day, los Genoveses, y Colón," *Temi Colombiani* (Genoa: ECIG, 1986), 363-71; Louis-André Vigneras, "The Cape Breton Landfall: 1494 or 1497. Note on a letter from John Day," *Canadian Historical Review* 38 (1957): 219-29; Louis-André Vigneras, "New Light on the 1497 Cabot Voyage to America," *Hispanic American Historical Review* 36 (1956): 503-9.

D'AZAMBUJA, DIOGO (1432-1518)
The commander of the fleet of eleven

vessels that King **John II** of **Portugal** sent to the Gold Coast of Africa in late 1481 to build the fort known as **San Jorge da Mina** (now Cape Coast Castle). The fort was constructed to protect trading interests in **gold** and **slaves** from other European countries and to dominate the natives. CC repeatedly claims, in marginal notes in his copy of **Pierre d'Ailly's** *Imago Mundi,* to have been at this site and presumably either sailed in D'Azambuja's fleet or traveled there soon after the fort was built.

Ref. *AOS*1 I, 53, 59 *n.*23.

DEGREE, LENGTH OF

CC concluded from his (notoriously inaccurate) experiments in sighting the sun with a **quadrant** that a degree of the earth's circumference was fifty-six and two-thirds Roman miles, in agreement with the geographer Afragan. This measurement is closely related to CC's conceptions of a world much smaller than the approximate 25,000-mile circumference now accepted.

Ref. *AOS*1 I, 68, *n.*26; S.E. Morison, "Columbus and Polaris," *American Neptune* 1 (1941): 128, *n.*72; G.E. Nunn, *The Geographical Conceptions of Columbus* (New York: American Geographical Society, 1924), 1-26.

DEMARCATION, LINE OF
The north-south line dividing the Spanish and Portuguese discoveries in both the Eastern and Western Hemispheres. Under the influence of King **Ferdinand,** whose aid had helped him rise in the Church, Pope Alexander VI issued five **papal bulls** on the new discoveries, favorable to **Spain** vis-à-vis **Portugal.** The third of these bulls, *Inter Caetera II* (1493; *see* **Carvajal, Bernardino de**), drew the famous demarcation line one hundred leagues west of the **Azores** which divided both eastern and western discoveries between Portugal and Spain, and negated the Portuguese interpretation of the earlier bull *Aeterni Regis* (Pope Sixtus IV, 1481) which, according to the Portuguese, gave them rights of discovery to everything south of the **Canary Islands.** The north-south line was later (1494) fixed by the Treaty of Tordesillas at forty-six degrees thirty minutes West **longitude.**

Ref. *AOS*1 II, 23-28; *AOS*2, 369-73; Edward Gaylord Bourne, "The History and Determination of the Line of Demarcation Established by Pope Alexander VI, between the Spanish and Portuguese Fields of Discovery and Colonization," *Yale Review* 1 (1892): 35-55; H. Van der Linden, "Alexander VI and the Demarcation of the Maritime and Colonial Domains of Spain and Portugal, 1493-1494," *American Historical Review* 22 (1916-17): 1-20.

DESEADA

See DESIRADE.

DESIRADE

An island to the east and to the windward of **Guadeloupe** in the **Lesser Antilles.** From the sixteenth through the nineteenth centuries, this was the recommended spot toward which sailing vessels aimed their course in sailing from Europe to the **West Indies.** The channels both north and south of this island lead ships between Guadeloupe and **Domenica** to protected waters west of the Lesser Antilles, whereas other routes lead either out of the **trade winds** or into treacherous waters. On his **Second Voyage,** CC hit this route perfectly (by either good luck or the great skill that characterized his **navigation** generally) and established it as the preferred route for the entire era of the sailing vessel. CC called the island Deseada.

Ref. *AOS*1 II, 67; *AOS*2, 404; S.E. Morison, *The Second Voyage of Christopher Columbus from Cádiz to Hispaniola and the Discovery of the Lesser Antilles* (Oxford: Clarendon, 1939).

DEZA, DIEGO DE (1444-1523)

A Dominican priest (later bishop of Palencia and Archbishop of **Seville**) who headed the college of St. Stephen at the University of Salamanca when the Spanish Royal Commission that heard and judged CC's **Enterprise of the Indies** met at the University from 1485 to 1487. Deza seems to have sympathized with CC and to have persuaded the commission not to reject the Enterprise outright even though they did not believe it practicable.

Ref. *AOS*1 I, 116-17; *AOS*2, 88, 666; Henry Vignaud, *Histoire Critique de la Grande Entreprise de Christophe Colomb,* vol. 1 (Paris: Welter, 1911), 569-99.

DIARIO

See JOURNAL OF THE FIRST VOYAGE.

DIAS, BARTHOLOMEW (ca. 1450-1500)

The commander of a Portuguese expedition to reach India by sailing east around Africa. The ships left **Lisbon** in the summer of 1487. Blown by a **storm** to a point well south of the Cape of Good Hope, they sighted land again 200 miles east of the Cape on 3 February 1488. After sailing northward along the east African coast for some time, the crews refused to continue and Dias reluctantly began the voyage home. The Cape, first seen by Europeans on the return voyage, was given the name "Good Hope" either by Dias or by King **John II.** Later Dias, or another mariner of the same name, was serving as master of the patrol ship that first confronted CC when he sailed the *Niña* into the Lisbon harbor, the estuary of the **Tagus River,** on his return from the **First Voyage** on 4 March 1493. Dias delivered a demand to CC on board the *Niña* to leave the ship and come aboard the patrol ship for questioning. CC refused, producing his credentials from **Isabel** and **Ferdinand** explaining the voyage and designating his admiral status. Dias and his captain backed down and, after a visit of about eleven days in **Portugal** as guest of King John II, CC was allowed to sail on to **Palos.**

Ref. *AOS1* I, 98-99, 265, 436; *AOS2*, 75-76, 341, 465-66; E.G. Ravenstein, "Voyages of Diogo Cao and Bartholomeu Dias," *Geographical Journal* 16 (1900): 638-49.

DIAZ DE ISLA, RUY (n.d.)
A Spanish physician who published a book (*Tractado contra el mal serpentino,* Seville, 1539) containing a clinical description of the symptoms of **syphilis** and an account of the outbreak of the great European syphilis epidemic of the 1490s in **Barcelona.** He claims that a pilot named Pinçón, presumably **Martín Alonso Pinzón** who died very shortly after returning to **Palos,** very likely had contracted the disease, and that CC's sailors or his **Indians** passed it along while they were in Barcelona in the spring of 1493.

Ref. *AOS1* II, 193-218; Francisco Guerra, "The Problem of Syphilis," *First Images of America,* vol.

2, ed. Fredi Chiapelli (Berkeley: University of California Press, 1976), 845-51; M. Lungonelli, "Colombo e il morbo Gallico," *Bolletino del Civico Istituto Colombiano* (Genoa) 1, no. 2 (1953): 51-64.

DOLDRUMS
A belt of calm weather on both sides of the equator between the belts of the north and south **trade winds.** The intense solar radiation striking this area generates **hurricanes** and other violent **storms** as well as extended periods without wind that can immobilize sailing ships for weeks. CC's fleet on the **Third Voyage** was becalmed in the doldrums east of the **Cape Verde Islands** from 15 to 22 July 1498, when the fleet drifted back into the trade winds.

Ref. *AOS1* II, 240-44; *AOS2*, 522-26.

DOMINICA
An island in the **Lesser Antilles,** just south of **Guadeloupe,** discovered by CC on his **Second Voyage.** Dominica is notable as the island on which the **Carib Indians** still survive, perhaps because their resistance to Europeans was so fierce that the early explorers left them alone and looked elsewhere for land, **slaves,** and plunder.

DRAGON, BOCAS DEL
Four channels of the northern egress of the **Gulf of Paria** into which the northern distributaries of the **Orino-**

co and the Rio Grande empty. They were named by CC, who discovered them on his **Third Voyage.** The channels are separated by reef-islands. *See* CHACACHACARE ISLAND.

Ref. *AOS1* II, 255-77; *AOS2*, 534-51.

DUDEM SIQUIDEM
See PAPAL BULLS.

DULMO, FERNÃO (n.d.)
A navigator of Terceira Island in the **Azores,** commissioned with João Estreito of **Madeira** by King **John II** of **Portugal** to seek the mythical Island(s) of the Seven Cities in the Atlantic by sailing west from Terceira. Nothing is known of how their voyage turned out, but the plan exhibits the error that CC avoided: their course would make them head into the prevailing westerlies. CC dropped south into the **trade winds,** which blew his 1492 fleet across to islands on the other side in thirty-nine days.

Ref. *AOS1* I, 97-100; *AOS2*, 74.

E

EAST INDIES

A term formerly assigned to the archipelago extending from just south of Singapore to just west of New Guinea, including the Indonesian islands of Java, Sumatra, Celebes, and the **Moluccas;** Borneo, divided between Indonesia and Malaysia; and many other islands. The term "East" distinguishes these islands from the **West Indies** in the Caribbean. The Moluccas, between Celebes and New Guinea, were a major source of the spices imported into Europe in the late Middle Ages. The term "**Spice Islands,**" applied indiscriminately to the whole archipelago by Europeans for many years, belongs properly to the Moluccas. The term "**Indies**"— from the early European association of the Spice Islands with India—was applied indiscriminately to both the West Indies and the East Indies until it became clear after **Magellan**'s voyage that the Indies discovered by CC were not identical with the Spice Islands.

EDEN, GARDEN OF

See **TERRESTRIAL PARADISE.**

EGG ISLAND

See **ELEUTHERA ISLAND.**

EGG STORY

An apocryphal tale of CC's resourcefulness in conversation, sometimes said to have happened in **Spain,** sometimes in the **Indies.** In one of the best accounts, CC is having breakfast with a group of courtiers while a guest in the palace of the Cardinal of Spain, Don **Pedro Gonzales de Mendoza.** Unable to endure any more adulation of the insufferably successful Genoese, one of the courtiers pointed out to CC that all he did was get his **ships** in the wind and sail west. "Anyone can do that," he concluded. In response, CC passed the disgruntled courtier a hard-boiled egg and invited him to stand it on its end. The courtier refused to try. CC then simply brought the round end of the egg down on the table hard enough to flatten the shell a bit, and so made the egg stand up. To this the courtier remarked deprecatingly, "Why, anyone can do it that way." CC answered, "It's the same with sailing to the Indies. Anyone can do it, when someone has shown him how." The story has been found in medieval accounts written before CC's day, attributed to other Europeans.

> Ref. *AOS*1 II, 15; *AOS*2, 361-62; Cesare De Lollis, *Cristoforo Colombo nella leggenda e nella storia* (Florence: Sansoni, 1969).

ELEUTHERA ISLAND

An island in the **Bahamas** northwest of **Cat Island** and northeast of New Providence and Andros Islands. The tiny Egg Island, as it is called, is one of several small islands extending in a southwest line from the northern extremity of Eleuthera. It is the northernmost island to be nominated by a serious nautical scholar as the site of CC's 1492 **landfall.** One interesting point in the argument is that Ponce de León, who measured the **latitude** of the island that he considered to be **San Salvador** (**Guanahani**) in 1513, recorded this latitude as twenty-five degrees forty minutes, very close to the latitude of Egg.

> Ref. A.B. Molander, "A New Approach to the Landfall," *Terrae Incognitae* 15 (1983): 113-49; A.B. Molander, *In the Wake of Columbus* (Detroit: Wayne State University Press, 1985), 113-49, reprint of the periodical.

EMANUEL I (1469-1521)

King of **Portugal** (1495-1521); also Manuel or Manoel. Brother-in-law of **John II** (reigned 1482-1495). Emanuel commissioned **Vasco da Gama**'s successful voyage to Calcutta (1497-99), which brought to fulfillment the long campaign of **Henry the Navigator** to reach the Far East and its spice trade by sailing south of Africa. The Portuguese empire in the east assembled by Emanuel collided with the Spanish expansion in the **New World** after CC's ambition of reaching the **Spice Islands** by sailing west was finally accomplished by **Magellan** in 1520.

ENCOMIENDAS

A system of quasi-serfdom established under CC in **Hispaniola** as a partial response to the **Roldán** rebellion in 1498. Originally known as *repartimientos,* the system allowed the European recipients of land grants to treat the native peoples on the land as their property, subject to whatever work the landowner gave them. The system, which spread to other Spanish holdings in the **New World,** contributed to the total destruction of the native population of Hispaniola and to the decimation of other concentrations of natives. The system began to decline about 1542.

> Ref. *AOS*1 II, 299.

ENGAÑO, CAPE

The easternmost point of **Hispaniola,** where the fleet of the **Second Voyage** made its **landfall.**

> Ref. *AOS*1 II, 90, 159, 182; *AOS*2, 422, 479.

ENGLAND

CC may have visited the English port of **Bristol,** especially if he traveled aboard vessels sent north by Genoese merchants with bases in **Lisbon,** such as the house of **di Negro.** These would have engaged in a three- or four-way trading project involving Portuguese wine, Bristol wool, and **Iceland** codfish. In a biography of his father, **Ferdinand Columbus** writes that CC observed fifty-foot tides in Iceland. Such tides are typical of Bristol but not Iceland; the detail might easily have been transferred to another port of call in the memory of CC's son.

After failing in **Portugal,** CC at some point sent his brother, **Bartholomew,** to offer the **Enterprise of the Indies** to King **Henry VII** of England, who refused it.

Ref. *EDA2*, 14-17, 39.

ENRÍQUEZ DE HARANA, BEATRIZ (n.d.)

A young woman of **Córdova,** an orphan under the guardianship of a cousin named Rodrigo Enríquez de Harana, father of Diego **de Harana,** who became the marshall of the fleet on CC's **First Voyage.** While CC was resident in Córdova around 1487 awaiting the report of the Royal Commission on his **Enterprise of the Indies,** Beatriz became his mistress (apparently with the approval of Rodrigo), and in August 1488 she bore him his second son and future biographer, **Ferdinand Columbus.** Some nineteenth-century enthusiasts for the **canonization** of CC, led by Roselly de Lorgues, tried to show that he had married Beatriz and that Ferdinand was born in wedlock; but the evidence to the contrary is conclusive. For example, CC took the trouble, after returning from the First Voyage, to have the Spanish monarchs legitimatize Ferdinand. Also, there is no evidence whatever that CC married Beatriz after the boy was born, and such a marriage would have been impossible after his return from the First Voyage with the ranks of knight, admiral, and viceroy. These made him a grandee, prohibited by Spanish law from marrying a commoner.

CC confided in his last years a sense of guilt at having dealt unjustly with Beatriz, whose only support seems to have been the small annuity he received from the crown as the prize for being the first to sight land at the time of the **landfall,** 12 October 1492.

Ref. *AOS1* I, 111-19, 429; *AOS2*, 83-85, 358, 668; José de la Torre y del Cerro, *Beatriz Enríquez de Harana y Cristóbal Colón* (Madrid: Compañia Iberoamericana de Publicaciones, 1933); Juan Manzano Manzano, *La legitimación de Hernando Colón* (Seville: University of Seville, 1960).

ENTERPRISE OF THE INDIES

"La Empresa de las Indias," the name associated with CC's project to sail west to discover a sea route to the **Indies.** CC sought sponsorship at the Portuguese, English, and French courts before succeeding in **Spain.**

EPHEMERIDES

See LUNAR ECLIPSE OF **1504.**

ERICSSON, LEIF (d. ca. 1020)

A Norse mariner, probably born in **Iceland,** who, in the accounts of the Norse Sagas, landed in Vinland (probably New England) about A.D. 1000, when he was blown off course during a voyage to Greenland. He thus is credited with discovering **America** almost 500 years before CC.

No doubt other Europeans landed in the Western Hemisphere at various times, and of course the Eskimos and **Indians,** Asiatic peoples, had come in prehistoric times. CC's distinction is not that he discovered the Western Hemisphere, but that he was responsible for opening it up to European settlement and culture.

Ref. *EDA*1 35-82, 347-48, 367, 489.

ESCALANTE, JUAN DE (d. 1519)

One of a number of mariners including **Amerigo Vespucci** and **Alonso de Hojeda,** whom the Spanish monarchs allowed to make voyages to the Western Hemisphere after CC was returned in chains to **Spain** at the end of the **Third Voyage.** These voyages

marked the end of CC's authority over the waters in the Spanish area of influence in the western Atlantic and in the Caribbean, as his arrest by **Bobadilla** in **Hispaniola** in the fall of 1500 marked the end of his viceroyship. CC was, nonetheless, allowed to retain the title of **Admiral of the Ocean.**

Ref. *AOS*1 II, 313.

ESCOBAR, DIEGO DE (n.d.)

The captain of a **caravel** that **Ovando** sent in March 1504, during the **Fourth Voyage,** to the site of CC's shipwreck in **Jamaica** to report on the situation of the admiral and his restless crews. Escobar delivered some wine and salt pork to CC and informed him that **Diego Méndez,** whom CC had sent to **Hispaniola** in a **canoe** to find aid, was seeking a ship in which to undertake the rescue. Escobar returned to report to Ovando without rescuing any of CC's people.

Ref. *AOS*1 II, 407-8; *AOS*2, 656-57.

ESCOBEDO, RODRIGO DE (d. ca. 1492)

The secretary of the fleet on CC's **First Voyage.** His duties would have been to conduct any diplomatic correspondence that might be necessary; none was. Escobedo was one of the group left at the fort of **Navidad** after the wreck of the *Santa María* and, according to **Bartolomé de Las Casas,** was a leader with **Pedro de Gutiérrez** of a gang of Spaniards who toured the island of **Hispaniola** raping and stealing, thus precipitating the massacre of the garrison at Navidad.

Ref. *AOS*1 I, 188-90, 301, 382-94, II, 95; *AOS*2, 146, 295.

ESDRAS

The name assigned to four Old Testament books in the Latin Vulgate Bible. The third and fourth of these are apocryphal. The first two books are called Ezra and Nehemiah in the King James English Protestant Bible; the third and fourth are called 1 and 2 Esdras in the King James Apocrypha. CC was partial to a passage in 4 Esdras 6:1, which suggested to medieval geographers that the world was six-sevenths dry land and one-seventh water. In the passage he found support for his belief that the voyage to Asia would be no more than about one-seventh of the circumference of the globe.

Ref. *AOS*1 I, 94*n.,* 123; *AOS*2, 71*n.,* 94; *Encyclopedia Britannica,* 11th ed., s.v. "Ezra, 3rd Book of."

ESPAÑOLA

The name given by CC in the 9 December 1492 entry of the *Journal of the First Voyage* to the island on which **Haiti** and the **Dominican Republic** are located. **Peter Martyr,** in his letter of 20 October 1494, latinized Española to **Hispaniola.**

Ref. *AOS*2, 283; *Raccolta di documenti e studi pubblicati dalla R. Commissione colombiana pel quarto centenario della scoperta dell'America,* vol. 3 (Rome: Ministro della Pubblica Istruzione, 1892-96), ii:43.

ESPINGARDA

An early musket made of a bronze or iron tube fastened to a stock of wood. CC carried these and crossbows as small arms on the **First Voyage.**

Ref. C. Fernández Duro, "Armamento de las carabelas de Colón," *El Centenario* (Madrid) 1 (1892): 197-207; J.F. Guillen Tato, *La carabela "Santa María," apuntes para su reconstitución* (Madrid: Ministerio de Marina, 1927), 110-22.

EVANGELISTA

The name given by CC to an island south of **Cuba** or to the westernmost part of Cuba when he decided to end his exploration of the southern Cuban shore on 13 June 1494, during the **Second Voyage. Bernáldez, Peter Martyr, Ferdinand Columbus,** and **Juan de La Cosa** give different locations for Evangelista. The name is derived from St. John the Evangelist.

Ref. *AOS*1 II, 160, *n.*1.

EXIMIAE DEVOTIONIS
See PAPAL BULLS.

F

FERDINAND V (1452-1516)

Spanish king of **Castile** and Léon (1474-1504), king of **Aragón** (as Ferdinand II; (1479-1516), king of Sicily (1468-1516), and king of Naples (1504-1516). Ferdinand was the first king of a united **Spain,** which he ruled jointly with **Isabel I** of Castile, from 1479 to 1504; together they were known as the **Catholic Monarchs.** Before Ferdinand inherited the crown of Aragón in 1479, he became joint monarch of Castile with his wife Isabel, ruling with her from 1474 until her death in 1504. After her death he continued to control Castile from 1504 until his death in 1516 as regent for his daughter Juana of Castile (1504-1555). Juana, being incompetent, ruled through regents throughout her life. After terminating a war with **Portugal** and subduing the strong-minded and individualistic nobles of Castile, the Catholic Monarchs resolved to bring to a conclusion the war with the **Moors** in the **Iberian Peninsula,** whose expulsion had been a Spanish Christian passion for 700 years. The final phase of the war was directed against the only remaining Moorish polity in the peninsula, the

kingdom of **Granada.** It was undoubtedly this war that, more than anything else, blocked the acceptance of CC's **Enterprise of the Indies** in the years following 1485, when CC came to Spain to propose it. The war dragged on until 2 January 1492 when Boabdil, king of Granada, surrendered to Ferdinand and Isabel. Promptly thereafter, Ferdinand and Isabel revived their interest in CC's Enterprise, and on 17 April 1492, signed the **Capitulations of 1492,** the contract that commissioned CC to sail west in search of the **Indies** and delineated his duties and prospective rewards as explorer.

Although Ferdinand and CC were in conflict over the latter's removal as viceroy and governor of **Hispaniola** in 1500, there is strong evidence that CC was always paid his one-tenth of the profits from the exploitation of the **West Indies.** Moreover, Ferdinand concurred with Isabel in bringing up CC's two sons as pages at court and approved the appointment of CC's son **Diego** as second **Viceroy of the Indies** and second **Admiral of the Ocean** after CC's death. Though **Bartolomé de Las Casas** (*Historia,* chap. 183) indicates that Isabel was more sympathetic to CC than Ferdinand, there is no indication that Ferdinand harbored a grudge against the mariner who had given Spain its new empire. *See* CAPITULATIONS OF 1492 and CATHOLIC MONARCHS.

Ref. Juan Gil, "Las cuentas de Cristóbal Colón," *Anuario de Estudios Americanos* (Seville) 41 (1984): 425-511; R.B. Merriman, *The Rise of the Spanish Empire in the Old World and the New,* vols. 1 and 2 (New York: Macmillan, 1936); Lee Anne Durham Seminario, *The History of the Blacks, The Jews and the Moors in Spain* (Madrid: Playor, S.A., 1975).

FERNÁNDEZ, ALEJO (d. ca. 1545)
A Spanish artist of **Córdova** who, in about 1520, made the famous painting "Our Lady of the Fair Winds," which includes, to the right of the virgin, a kneeling figure with grey hair and beard, fair complexion, aquiline nose, and long face, that is sometimes said to represent CC. A reproduction of the painting serves as the frontispiece of Samuel Eliot Morison's *Admiral of the Ocean Sea* (Boston: Little, Brown, 1942).

FERNÁNDEZ, DR. GARCÍA (n.d.)
A physician of the town of **Huelva** near **Palos** whose testimony in **Los Pleitos** in 1513 helped establish CC's relationship with the Franciscan friars at **La Rábida.** Dr. Fernández's account has CC arriving at the friary with his small son in 1491 to ask for a cup of water for the thirsty child. The simplicity and pathos of the act were said to have won over the Franciscans. Since **Diego Columbus** would have been too old for this in 1491 and since his son **Ferdinand Columbus** was less than three at the time, CC scholars, beginning with Washington Irving, have concluded that Fernández conflated two incidents in his mind— the arrival of CC with Diego in 1485, and his return to get the boy in 1491. By the latter date, CC had despaired of aid in **Spain** and was about to set out for France to join his brother **Bartholomew,** who was already there to propose the **Enterprise of the Indies.**

Ref. *AOS*1 I, 108, 133; *AOS*2, 80, 99.

FERNÁNDEZ, GARCÍA (n.d.)
A steward on board the *Pinta* during CC's **First Voyage.** His statements help establish **Martín Alonso Pinzón** as a much-admired mariner in **Palos** whose influence with his townsmen was responsible for CC's success in recruiting excellent crews for the fleet of discovery.

Ref. *AOS*2, 136, 147; Angel Ortega, *La Rábida: historia documental crítica,* vols. 2 and 3 (Seville: Editorial de San Antonio, 1925-26), 2: 161-62, 3: 30-175.

FERNÁNDEZ DE CORONEL, PEDRO
See **CORONEL, PEDRO FERNÁNDEZ DE.**

FERNANDINA ISLAND

An island in the **Bahamas** discovered by CC on 16 October 1492, identified by Morison as the one now called **Long Island,** although it does not now present the flat appearance that CC described in his *Journal.* Other scholars explain this difference as evidence that Morison's account of CC's route through the Bahamas is incorrect.

Ref. *AOS1* I, 317-18; Louis De Vorsey and John Parker, eds., *In the Wake of Columbus: Islands and Controversy* (Detroit: Wayne State University Press, 1985).

FERRER, JAIME (n.d.)

A Spanish lapidary whose reputation in cosmography was such that he was consulted by the sovereigns in the matter of the Line of **Demarcation** between Spanish and Portuguese areas of influence in the Atlantic. Before the **Third Voyage,** Ferrer's advice to CC that gems and **gold** were to be found near the equator led the admiral to follow the **latitude** of Sierra Leone, far south of the **Canary Islands,** from where CC had set out across the Atlantic on his first two voyages. This more southerly route enabled him to land at **Trinidad** and to discover South **America** on this Third Voyage.

Ref. *AOS1* I, 254, II, 233-34; *AOS2,* 515-16; John Boyd Thacher, *Christopher Columbus: His Life, His Work, His Remains,* 3 vols. (New York: Putnam, 1903-4), 2: 194-97, 366-67.

FERRO ISLAND

The westernmost of the **Canary Islands,** under the acting captaincy of **Beatriz de Bobadilla y Peraza** during the time of CC's voyages. The dates on which the fleets of discovery passed Ferro on the four voyages are: 9 September 1492; 13 October 1493; 21 June 1498; and 26 May 1502.

Ref. *AOS1* I, 266, II, 59, 237, 323.

FIESCHI, BARTOLOMEO (n.d.)

The Genoese who was reported to have served commendably with CC on the **Fourth Voyage** as captain of the *Vizcaina.* Fieschi commanded one of the two **canoes** that CC sent to **Hispaniola** for aid when he and his crews were marooned on **Jamaica.** The other canoe was commanded by **Diego Méndez;** the expedition succeeded in securing rescue for CC and the rest of his men. Fieschi's account of this canoe trip is related by CC's son **Ferdinand** in his biography of his father. Fieschi, like Méndez, was present at the death of CC in **Valladolid** on 20 May 1506.

Ref. *AOS1* II, 327, 420; *AOS2,* 586, 647-50, 669; Ferdinand Columbus, *The Life of the Admiral Christopher Columbus,* ed. and trans. Benjamin Keen (New Brunswick: Rutgers University Press, 1959).

FIRST VOYAGE OF DISCOVERY

3 August 1492-15 March 1493. CC's voyage, departing from **Palos,** during which he discovered the **Bahamas, Cuba,** and **Hispaniola.** CC's plans for this trip, which he called his **Enterprise of the Indies,** was offered first to **John II** of **Portugal** in about 1484 and perhaps again in 1488, both times unsuccessfully. **Ferdinand** and **Isabel** of **Spain,** after delaying CC from 1485 until 1492 in order to complete their war against the **Moors** before undertaking new ventures, authorized the voyage in the **Capitulations of 1492.** The monarchs authorized three **ships** and ordered the city of Palos not only to turn over two **caravels** owed to the crown, but also to aid in preparing the voyage. The crews were assembled with help from **Martín Alonso Pinzón,** who then commanded the *Pinta,* one of the two caravels furnished by Palos. The other caravel was the *Niña,* owned by **Juan Niño.** The third ship was a larger ship, a nao called the *Santa María.* It was owned by **Juan de La Cosa,** who brought it to Palos from **Seville.** After a shakedown cruise to the **Canary Islands,** the point of entry into the Atlantic crossing, CC had repairs and adjustments made to the two caravels and on 6 September departed from the island of **Gomera.**

CC arrived in the Bahamas at the island of **Guanahani** on 12 October 1492. He explored the Bahamas, Cuba, and Hispaniola until 24 December, when the *Santa María* ran aground and broke up in the surf. Aided by friendly **Indians,** CC and his crew got the supplies and timber ashore and built a makeshift fort called **Navidad,** where CC left some forty of his total crew of 100 in the first Spanish colony in the **New World.** On 16 January 1493 the *Niña,* commanded by CC, and the *Pinta*, commanded by Pinzón, sailed for Spain on the return voyage. After a stormy crossing and brief sojourns in other ports on the Atlantic seaboard (*Niña* at **Lisbon,** *Pinta* at **Bayona**), the two ships arrived at their home port of Palos on 15 March 1493.

Ref. *AOS*1 II, 1-5; *AOS*2, 109-359; *JOD,* 41-179; Kirkpatrick Sale, *The Conquest of Paradise: Christopher Columbus and the Columbian Legacy* (New York: Knopf, 1990), 7-9, 10-16, 16-18, 18-21, 22-26, 27, 47-50, 56-63, 64-68, 69-73, 92-121, 124, 186*n.*, 191, 220, 235, 262, 358, 379*n.*1.

FLECHA, CABO DE LA

Spanish for "Cape of the Arrow." Prominent cape on the island of **St. Croix** in the northern part of the **Lesser Antilles.** Near this cape, at the mouth of Salt River Bay, CC and his mariners engaged **Indians,** perhaps **Caribs,** in the first battle between the Spanish and the native Americans on 13 November 1493, during the **Second Voyage.**

Ref. *AOS*1 II, 85.

FLECHAS, LAS
Spanish for "The Arrows." Name of a cape on the northeast shore of **Hispaniola** and of the bay or gulf into which it juts. At this point on 13 January 1493, just before the departure of the *Niña* and *Pinta* for **Spain,** CC's crew, ashore to seek supplies, had a minor skirmish with the **Ciguayan** natives and narrowly avoided a battle. This was the closest CC came to a serious battle on the **First Voyage.**

Ref. *AOS*1 I, 399-403; *AOS*2, 311-12.

FLORES
One of the two westernmost **Azores** islands, discovered in 1452 by **Diogo de Teive.**

Ref. *AOS*1 I, 41, 411-13.

FONSECA, JUAN DE RODRIGUEZ
See **RODRIGUEZ DE FONSECA, JUAN.**

FONTANABUONA
The valley northeast of **Genoa** in which CC's grandfather was born and from which he emigrated to **Quinto.** *See* **COLOMBO FAMILY.**

FONTANAROSSA, SUZANNA
See **COLOMBO FAMILY.**

FOURTH VOYAGE OF DISCOVERY
3 April 1502-7 November 1504. A fleet of four **caravels,** *Capitana, Bermuda, Gallega, Vizcaina,* with a total crew of 135, embarked from **Seville,** made the usual stop at the **Canary Islands** on 20 May, sailed for the **Indies** on 25 May and entered the **Lesser Antilles** at **Martinique** on 15 June after the speediest of CC's Atlantic crossings (twenty-one days). At **Santo Domingo** on the south coast of **Hispaniola,** although forbidden by the sovereigns to set foot on the island, CC requested permission from the governor, **Ovando,** to take refuge from an oncoming **hurricane.** Denied permission to enter the harbor, CC took shelter with his caravels off the southern shore of Hispaniola, where all four **ships** weathered the **storm** successfully. A treasure fleet from Santo Domingo, dispatched despite CC's message about the hurricane, was struck by the full force of the storm; nineteen ships were lost with all hands, six others were sunk but left survivors, and four more limped back to Santo Domingo. The only ship to reach **Spain** was the *Aguja* bearing a consignment of **gold** for CC which reached Seville safely.

Steering between **Jamaica** and **Cuba,** CC proceeded on his mission to explore for a strait leading to the Indian Ocean and reached central

America at **Bonacca** Island off the coast of **Honduras** about 30 July. CC took the coastline to be the shore of the **Golden Chersonese** (presumably the southward-thrusting extension of Asia comprising Indo-China and the Malay Peninsula, as this extension was understood by Europeans). CC spent the next two and a half months with the squadron sailing south along this Caribbean coast in ceaseless rainstorms, searching vainly for the strait.

He finally stopped in a region of **Panama** that the natives called **Veragua.** After explorations and an abortive attempt to settle a colony, his ships rotting from the attack of worms on the timbers, CC abandoned the *Gallega* and sailed with three still-floating ships on 16 April 1503 for Hispaniola. He abandoned the *Vizcaina* on 23 April, touched Cuba, and then on 25 June beached his two remaining ships, *Capitana* and *Bermuda,* at **St. Ann's Bay** on the north shore of Jamaica to keep them from sinking.

The admiral and his crew were stranded on Jamaica for more than a year until rescued on 29 June 1504 by a caravel secured in Santo Domingo by CC's heroic gentleman-volunteer **Diego Méndez.** Méndez, with **Bartolomeo Fieschi** and two **canoes** rowed by Jamaican Indians, had crossed the passage to Hispaniola against the **trade winds.** CC then embarked for Spain in a chartered ship with the twenty-one of his surviving crewmen who decided not to stay in Hispaniola. The ship reached Seville on 7 November 1504, ending CC's career at sea.

Ref. *AOS*2, 575-659; *JOD,* 314-98; Kirkpatrick Sale, *The Conquest of Paradise: Christopher Columbus and the Columbian Legacy* (New York: Knopf, 1990), 184, 186*n.*, 188, 192-211, 225, 381*n.*3.

FUERTEVENTURA ISLAND
See **CANARY ISLANDS.**

FUNCHAL
The capital of the **Madeira** archipelago off the northwest coast of Africa, an archipelago controlled by **Portugal** from early in the fifteenth century. Funchal, located on the southeast shore of the island of Madeira, was a sugar-exporting center in the late 1470s when CC, as seagoing agent for the **Lisbon** office of the Genoese importing-exporting firm of **di Negro,** attempted in 1478 to purchase a shipment of sugar for the associated Genoese firm of **Centurione.** Because of some defect in the arrangements, CC had not been given enough money to purchase the whole shipment of sugar and ultimately had to testify in court in **Genoa** about the resulting misunderstanding between the Centurione firm and the di Negro firm. CC's testimony, given on 25 August 1479 and reported in the

Assereto Document, has him claiming to be a citizen of Genoa and makes him about twenty-eight years old at the time. During the years from 1476 to 1485, when CC was a Portuguese resident, he and his wife, **Felipa Perestrello e Moniz,** apparently lived for a time in Funchal, accounting for the enthusiastic reception that he received from the citizens when his fleet visited there in 1498 during the **Third Voyage,** according to **Bartolomé de Las Casas**'s summary of CC's journal.

Ref. *AOS*1 I, 39-60; *JOD,* 259-63, a translation of Las Casas's summary of CC's *Journal* of the 1498 voyage; Alberto A. Sarmento, *Ensaios Historicos da Minha Terra* (Funchal, 1939); Fernando Augusto da Silva, *A Lombada dos Esmeraldos na Ilha da Madeira* (Funchal, 1933).

G

GALICIA

A maritime province in northwest **Spain** just north of the Portuguese border. On its Atlantic coast is located **Bayona,** where **Martín Alonso Pinzón** landed the *Pinta* in late February or early March 1493 after the crossing from **Hispaniola** on the **First Voyage.**

GALLEGA

A popular nickname for Castilian ships in CC's day, derived from the name of the maritime province of **Galicia.** Three **ships** in CC's fleets bore the name, either as a commissioned name or as a nickname: the **carrack** *Santa María* of the **First Voyage,** wrecked and destroyed off **Haiti** on Christmas Eve 1492; the carrack *Galicia* or *Gallega* of the **Second Voyage;** and a **caravel** of CC's fleet in the **Fourth Voyage** abandoned at **Belén.** *See* **SHIPS, CC'S.**

Ref. *AOS*1 I, 155, II, 55, 320; John Boyd Thacher, *Christopher Columbus: His Life, His Work, His Remains,* 3 vols. (New York and London: Putnam, 1903-4), 1: 569-72.

GALLEY

A Mediterranean cargo and combat vessel of the late medieval and early Renaissance period, driven chiefly by oars but using sails for auxiliary propulsion. Sometimes galleys were used in the Atlantic, as in the convoy of late summer 1476, sent by Genoese firms to trade along the English Channel. Some historians think CC was a mariner in this convoy on a sailing ship, the *Bechalla*, not a galley.

Ref. *AOS*1 I, xx-xxi, 31-32.

GALWAY

A city in western **Ireland** where CC made port, perhaps on a Portuguese voyage, in the winter of 1476/77. CC remarked in the handwritten notes in two of the books he owned that he had seen the bodies of a man and a woman, both of strange appearance, in boats adrift in the Atlantic at Galway; he assumed that they had floated across from the **Indies.**

Ref. *AOS*1 I, 33; *AOS*2, 25; *Raccolta di documenti e studi pubblicati dalla R. Commissione colombiana pel quarto centenario della scoperta dell'America,* vol. 1 (Rome:

Ministro della Pubblica Istruzione, 1892-96), 299, 395.

GAMA, VASCO DA (ca. 1469-1524)
The Portuguese commander who, in his voyage of 1497 to 1499, achieved the long-standing ambition of the House of Avis to reach India and open up the spice trade by sailing south of Africa. On the **Fourth Voyage,** CC carried a letter from the Spanish monarchs introducing him to da Gama, who was en route to India for a second time. The sovereigns, still believing the **West Indies** to be the **East Indies,** obviously hoped that CC would find the strait leading to the Indian Ocean and return to **Spain** south of Africa.

Ref. *AOS2*, 178, 187, 340, 348, 582.

GARCÍA, BARTOLOMÉ (n.d.)
A boatswain on the *Niña* of the **First Voyage,** who also sailed on the **Second** and **Fourth Voyages.**

Ref. *AOS1* I, 189, 192, II, 321; Alicia Bache Gould, *Nueva Lista Documentada de los Tripulantes de Colón en 1492,* ed. José M. de la Peña (Madrid: Real Academia de la Historia, 1984).

GARDEN OF THE QUEEN
See QUEEN'S GARDEN.

GARZA
A **caravel** of the **Third Voyage.** *See* SHIPS, **CC's.**

GENOA
The city in the Italian maritime province of **Liguria** where CC grew up. Closely hemmed in against the Mediterranean by the western **Alps,** Genoa was entirely dependent on the sea and the trade offered by the sea. During much of the medieval period, it had been a close rival of Venice for dominance of European trade in the Mediterranean and, in the early and middle fifteenth century, held trading colonies in the Aegean and on the Black Sea for the purpose of cultivating Oriental trade. Although in CC's day Genoa's commercial activity was in decline, it was by no means dead, and CC was associated throughout his life with three of the most prominent trading companies, those operated by the **di Negro, Centurione,** and **Spinola** families. He seems to have been aboard at least one of the two large expeditions that the di Negro and Spinola firms sent to the defense of the Genoese colony at **Chios** in the Aegean in the early 1470s. Although many other communities have challenged Genoa's claim to be CC's home, scores of fifteenth-and sixteenth-century documents exist in which CC is identified as Genoese. In 1931 the city published a monumental collection of these documents. So overwhelming is this proof that no responsible scholar since that time has denied CC's Genoese origin.

Ref. *AOS2*, 7-19, 22-23, 37, 513;

City of Genoa, *Christopher Co-lumbus: Documents and Proofs of his Genoese Origin* (Genoa: Insti-tuto d'Arti Grafiche, 1931); P.E. Taviani, *La Genovesità di Colombo* (Genoa: ECIG, 1987).

GERALDINI, ALESSANDRO (1455-1525)

A Genoese who met CC at **Granada** in 1492. In 1522 he became the first bishop of **Santo Domingo.** In his *Itinerarium,* written around 1522, he made one of the many contemporary references to CC as a Genoese.

Ref. *AOS1* I, 8; *AOS2,* 97, 99-100, 384, 420-21, 663.

GIOVO, PAOLO (1480-1552)

The bishop, humanist, and art collec-tor who assembled portraits of fa-mous persons in his villa on Lake Como in northern Italy. For some years after 1551 this collection in-cluded a portrait of CC, often identi-fied with the De Orchi portrait that now hangs in the Giovo Museum at Como. The De Orchi portrait, in some ways the most impressive of the fif-teenth-century paintings and etchings of CC, matches what is known of CC's appearance except that it has brown eyes (according to **Bartolomé de Las Casas,** his eyes were blue). However, since there is no known surviving authentic likeness of CC (whose portrait may never have been painted), the actual resemblance of CC's face to the portrait in the Giovo Museum is in doubt.

Ref. *AOS2,* 48; John Boyd Thacher, *Christopher Columbus: His Life, His Work, His Remains,* vol. 3 (New York: Putnam, 1903-4, re-print, New York: AMS, Kraus, 1967), 1-79.

GIUSTINIANI, AGOSTINO (1470-1536)

The Genoese scholar whose *Psalter-ium* of 1516 contains (in a note) a succinct life of CC, calling the navi-gator a Genoese. In 1537 Giustiniani, in his *Annals of Genoa,* refers to CC's bequest to the **Bank of St. George** in **Genoa.**

Ref. *AOS1* I, 7, 21.

GLASS

See AMPOLETTA.

GOLD

CC, in his *Journal of the First Voy-age* and elsewhere in his writings, showed an extraordinary interest in finding gold in the **Indies** and dili-gently sought a mine during his voy-ages. It is clear that he felt he had to find a generous source of gold in order to justify his voyage. Although the natives of the **Bahamas** and **Hispaniola** gave him a limited amount of gold in the form of body decora-tions, masks, and so on, and some gold was found in Hispaniola before 1500, especially as small nuggets in the river beds, no extensive source was located on the island until 1500. Beyond CC's desire to demonstrate the value of his discovery in such an unmistakable way, it is not completely clear how much his interest in gold was motivated by his genuine and frequently expressed desire to subsidize a crusade to recover Jerusalem, and how much was due to his wish to accumulate personal wealth. Because the **Capitulations of 1492** granted him one-tenth of all the profits deriving from his discoveries, discovery of a rich source of gold would have made him very wealthy. It was a curious aspect of CC's interest in gold that he appeared to have felt that the warmth of the **West Indies,** whose **latitude** he at one point miscalculated as forty-two degrees by reading his instrument wrong, was due to the presence of large deposits of gold.

Ref. *AOS*1 II, 435; *JOD,* 99, 37-187, 292-95.

GOLDEN CHERSONESE

The name that the classical cosmographer **Ptolemy** (Claudius Ptolemaeus, second century A.D) gave to the Malay Peninsula. CC seems to have thought that the Central American isthmus was the Golden Chersonese and on the **Fourth Voyage** sought a strait south of it leading to the Indian Ocean.

Ref. *AOS*1 II, 139-40, 344-45.

GOMERA

An island in the western part of the **Canary** archipelago, ruled at the beginning of the 1490s by **Beatriz de Bobadilla y Peraza,** whom CC visited in Gomera on the **First Voyage**

and the **Second,** and whom he may have known in **Spain** at some point. Gomera had been ruled in the early 1480s by Hernán de Peraza, member of a Spanish family long active in the conquest and settlement of the archipelago. When Peraza was brought to Spain to face charges of murdering another Spanish conquistador, Juan Rejón, the charges were dropped on condition that he marry Beatriz, one of **Isabel's** ladies-in-waiting and cousin of the other Beatriz de Bobadilla, the **Marquesa de Moya,** who was a close friend and confidant of Queen Isabel. Beatriz, who was thus forced to marry Hernán de Peraza, was *persona non grata* to Isabel because she had become King **Ferdinand's** mistress at court.

Ref. R.B. Merriman, *The Rise of the Spanish Empire in the Old World and in the New,* vol. 2 (New York: Macmillan, 1936), chap. 16 *passim;* Antonio Rumeu de Armas, "Cristóbal Colón y Beatriz de Bobadilla en las antevísperas del descubrimiento," *El Museo Canario* (Las Palmas) 75-76 (1960): 255-79.

GORBALAN, GINES DE (n.d.)

A captain of a **ship** on CC's **Second Voyage,** second in command to **Alonso de Hojeda** in the expedition that CC sent on 6 January 1494 to explore the inland of **Hispaniola,** only four days after the fleet landed and the Spaniards began to settle at **Isabela.** The expedition, comprising a score of men or more, crossed the northern mountain ridge into the central valley and found mountain streams coming down from the range the natives called **Cibao.** Assured there was much **gold** in the Cibao by natives who gave Hojeda several large nuggets, the expedition returned to Isabela on 20 January. Gorbalan, however, explored further on his own, seeking the **cacique Caonabó,** but decided to return without finding him after seeing further evidence of gold in the Cibao. He reached Isabela on 21 January 1494.

Ref. *AOS1* II, 56, 102-4; *AOS2,* 396, 431-33.

GORDA

The **caravel** on which CC was sent home from **Santo Domingo** as a prisoner by **Francisco de Bobadilla** in 1500. The ship had been sent to **Hispaniola** in a fleet bearing provisions in 1498, part of the **Third Voyage.** *See* SHIPS, CC's.

Ref. *AOS1* II, 232, 303, 309; *AOS2,* 571, 575.

GORRICIO, FRAY GASPAR (n.d.)

The Carthusian monk at the monastery of **Las Cuevas** in **Seville** who received CC in chains in 1500 when he reached the city from **Hispaniola,** and who was an old and devoted friend of CC and his family. He was one of CC's chief correspondents toward the end of the admiral's life; a number of the letters survive.

Ref. *AOS2,* 75-78; Manuel Serrano y Sanz, "Notes on Fray Gaspar Gorricio," *Boletin de la Real Academia de la Historia* 97 (1930): 158-70.

GRACIA, RIO DE

A river in northern **Hispaniola** which **Martín Alonso Pinzón** discovered and named for himself during the period in November-January 1493 when he left the fleet of the **First Voyage** and explored on his own in the *Pinta.* When CC became aware of this, he changed the name to Rio de Gracia.

Ref. *AOS1* I, 398.

GRANADA

A city in southern Andalusia, **Spain,** capital from 1238 to 1492 of the kingdom of the same name and the last refuge of the **Moors** who, after dominating the **Iberian Peninsula** since the early eighth century, were gradually driven south by the resurgent Christian population. When CC came to Spain in 1485 seeking support for his **Enterprise of the Indies,** the **Catholic Monarchs** were preoccupied with their war with Granada, and he was unable to get acceptance for his project until after Granada fell on 2 January 1492, ending seven centuries of Moorish hegemony in the peninsula. Shortly thereafter, the sovereigns heard his suit again and approved it.

Ref. *AOS1* I, 106-45; Juan Manzano Manzano, *Cristóbal Colón: Siete años decisivos de su vida, 1485-1492* (Madrid: Ediciones Cultura Hispanica, 1964).

GRAND CANARY ISLAND

The large central island of the **Canary** archipelago, conquered by the Spanish in a series of campaigns in the late 1470s and early 1480s. CC's *Pinta* and perhaps the *Niña* stopped for repairs at the capital, **Las Palmas,** after the first leg of the **First Voyage** from **Palos.**

Ref. *AOS*1 I, 210-14; R.B. Merriman, *The Rise of the Spanish Empire in the Old World and the New,* vol. 2 (New York: Macmillan, 1936), chap. 16 *passim.*

GRAND CARDINAL OF SPAIN

See MENDOZA, DON PEDRO GONZALES DE.

GRAND TURK ISLAND

At the southern end of the **Bahamas,** Grand Turk has most of the characteristics CC ascribed to **Guanahani,** the island on which he made his **landfall** on 12 October 1492. Other islands meet many of these criteria, most notably **San Salvador** (Watlings), which is the favorite among scholars who have written on the question. From Grand Turk, however, many islands are visible, a fact that corresponds to CC's remark in his *Journal*, in which he claimed to see "so many islands [from Guanahani] that I could not decide where to go first." This is not true of San Salvador Island.

Ref. *JOD,* 68, a passage in *Journal;* John Parker, "The Columbus Landfall Problem: A Historical Perspective," *Terrae Incognitae* 15 (1983): 1-28; R.H. Power, "The Discovery of Columbus's Island Passage to Cuba, October 12-27, 1492," *Terrae Incognitae* 15 (1983): 151-72.

GREATER ANTILLES

The part of the **West Indies** comprising **Puerto Rico, Hispaniola, Cuba,** and **Jamaica;** called "greater" because those islands in the archipelago east and south of Puerto Rico (the **Lesser Antilles**) are all much smaller than any of these four islands.

GREAT INAGUA

An island about eighty miles northeast of the easternmost point of **Cuba,** discovered by **Martín Alonso Pinzón** in the *Pinta* during the **First Voyage.** Morison identifies this island as **Babeque,** the name used by Cuban natives whom CC and his party met in November 1492.

Ref. *AOS*1 I, 343-78, 396; *JOD,* 41-179, entries of the *Journal* for October-January.

GRENADA

An island north of **Trinidad** at the southern end of the **Lesser Antilles.** Morison identifies Grenada as the island of **Asunción,** which CC sighted and named on the **Third Voyage** after he emerged from the **Gulf of Paría** on 13 August 1498.

Ref. *AOS*1 II, 275-77.

GROMET

A term used to designate a ship's boy or an ordinary seaman in Castilian ships of CC's day.

Ref. *AOS*1 I, 185; *AOS*2, 143.

GUACANAGARÍ (d. 1499)

Also rendered "Guacanagaric." The **Taino** chieftain or **cacique** of Marien in **Hispaniola** who aided CC in removing the cargo from the *Santa María* when it ran aground off the north shore of **Haiti** on 24 December 1492. Guacanagarí was reportedly much impressed with CC and evidently much embarrassed when CC, on his return in 1493, saw that his colony of **Navidad,** founded in a fort constructed from the timbers of the *Santa María,* had been massacred by angry native people of the island. Guacanagarí denied implication in the massacre and remained loyal to CC after the other natives had turned against the Spaniards. According to **Las Casas,** Guacanagarí eventually fled from the harsh conditions imposed by the Spaniards and died in exile in the mountains.

Ref. *AOS*1 I, 380-95, II, 91-95, 165-70; *AOS*2, 294-96, 302-7, 423-27; Bartolomé de Las Casas, *Popery Truly Display'd in Its Bloody Colours; or A Faithful Narrative of the Horrid and Unexampled Massacres, Butcheries, and All Manner of Cruelties, That Hell and Malice Could Invent, Committed by the Popish Spanish Party on the Inhabitants of West-India. . . .* (London: R. Hewson, 1689), 9; Kirkpatrick Sale, *The Conquest of Paradise: Christopher Columbus and the Columbian Legacy* (New York: Knopf, 1990), 114-18, 120-21.

GUADALQUIVIR RIVER

A major Spanish river mainly in Andalusia along which are situated the cities of **Córdova, Seville,** and **Cádiz.** The roadstead of **Sanlúcar de Barrameda** near Cádiz became the chief locale for the departure and return of **New World** fleets.

GUADALUPE

A town in the Castilian province of Estremadura, locale of a Jeronymite monastery and its gothic church containing the shrine of Our Lady of Guadelupe, to whom mariners were especially devoted. CC presumably named the island of **Guadeloupe** (Spanish, *Guadalupe*) in the **Lesser Antilles** for the shrine in response to a request by the monks to name an island for their patroness.

Ref. *AOS*1 II, 52-53; *AOS*2, 392-94, 507.

GUADELOUPE

An island in the **Lesser Antilles** that CC discovered on the **Second Voyage.** According to the biography of

CC by his son **Ferdinand Columbus,** it was named for Our Lady of Guadalupe at the request of the monks; the Spanish form *Guadalupe* was altered to the current spelling after the French occupation. On the Second Voyage, CC's route into the **West Indies** between Guadeloupe and **Dominica** proved to be the best ever discovered and was the standard route for sailing vessels until they were displaced by steamships.

Ref. *AOS1* II, 60; *AOS2*, 407-10, 498-99; Ferdinand Columbus, *The Life of the Admiral Christopher Columbus,* ed. and trans. Benjamin Keen (New Brunswick: Rutgers University Press, 1959), chap. 46 *passim.*

GUANAHANI

The native name for the island that CC called **San Salvador,** site of the **landfall** on 12 October 1492. According to CC's *Journal,* the island was "large"; populated by naked people; forested and extensively cultivated; contained a lagoon in the middle; and had "a harbor to hold all the ships in Christendom." Moreover, CC said that when he departed he "made sail, and saw so many islands that I could not decide where to go first." This description of CC's San Salvador is the only remaining clue to the identity of the island. The difficulty of assigning all these characteristics to any of the **Bahama** islands has precipitated the landfall controversy. No island in the Bahamas that can be shown to have exhibited these characteristics at the time, and that is not blocked from eastern access by other islands, can be excluded as a candidate.

Ref. *JOD,* 64-69; John Parker, "The Columbus Landfall Problem: A Historical Perspective," *Terrae Incognitae* 15 (1983): 1-28.

GUANCHES

The aboriginal peoples of the **Canary Islands.** The Guanches were conquered by the Spaniards in a series of campaigns that foreshadowed the Spanish conquest of the native populations in the **New World.**

Ref. R.B. Merriman, *The Rise of the Spanish Empire in the Old World and the New,* vol. 2 (New York: Macmillan, 1936), chap. 16.

GUANTANAMO BAY

A large natural harbor on the southwest coast of **Cuba,** currently the site of a major U.S. naval station. CC discovered the bay on 30 April 1494 during the **Second Voyage** while he was exploring the southern coast, partly to determine whether Cuba was part of the Asiatic mainland.

Ref. *AOS1* II, 120-21; *AOS2*, 448-50.

GUARIONEX (d. 1502)

An **Indian cacique** of Magua in **Hispaniola** who joined the **Roldán** revolt in 1497. He was captured by

Bartholomew Columbus and held until 1502, when he was placed on board the flagship of the treasure fleet that Ovando dispatched to Spain in June 1502, despite CC's warning that a severe storm was imminent. Guarionex was drowned when the ship went down in the storm, along with the ship's captain, Antonio de Torres, and Bobadilla, the representative of the crown who had sent CC home in chains in 1500.

Ref. *AOS*1 II, 174, 296, 325; *AOS*2, 492; Bartolomé de Las Casas, *Popery Truly Display'd in Its Bloody Colours; or A Faithful Narrative of the Horrid and Unexampled Massacres, Butcheries, and All Manner of Cruelties, That Hell and Malice Could Invent, Committed by the Popish Spanish Party on the Inhabitants of West-India. . . .* (London: R. Hewson, 1689), 8-9.

GUATIGUANA (n.d.)

An Indian cacique of Hispaniola, imprisoned and marked for slavery at the time CC sent 500 Indians from Isabela in early 1495 to sell as slaves in Spain. He escaped and thus avoided the slave transports that sailed on 24 February. Guatiguana marshalled a considerable army of Tainos to resist the Spaniards, but on 27 March was routed by the Spanish infantry and cavalry under Alonso de Hojeda and Bartholomew Columbus.

Ref. *AOS*1 II, 169-71; *AOS*2, 487-88; Bartolomé de Las Casas, *Historia de las Indias,* 3 vols., ed. Agustín Millares Carlo (Mexico City and Buenos Aires: Fondo de Cultura Económica, 1951). chap. 104 *passim.* revised in 1972; with an introduction by Lewis Hanke.

GUAYMI INDIANS

The Indian people who inhabited Central America from Chiriqui Lagoon in Costa Rica to what is now the modern Canal Zone. CC's men encountered them during the Fourth Voyage. One of the Guaymi Indians, Quibián, was a cacique who opened his village to CC's brother Bartholomew and some sixty-eight men, who proceeded to explore the coast for gold and possible settlement sites. Diego Méndez and Rodrigo de Escobar on one occasion visited Quibián. After a reportedly friendly dinner, they returned to CC alleging that the Guaymis planned to kill the Spaniards. CC decided Quibián and the others in the village, including women and children, should be taken prisoner. Some of the Guaymis taken prisoner subsequently hung themselves from deck beams aboard the *Santiago.*

Ref. *AOS*1 II, 343-44, 351-53, 367-76; *AOS*2, 610, 623-31; Henry F. Pittier, *National Geographic* 23 (1912): 640.

GUINEA

The name given in CC's day to that portion of the west African coast where the shoreline turns west toward the Congo from its generally north-south direction south of Morocco. On this coast the Portuguese built the castle of Le **Mina** in 1482 to protect their trading interests in the area. CC, while sailing on Portuguese ships in the early 1480s, visited the Guinea coast. He referred to these visits frequently in the marginal notes he wrote in books he owned, particularly the *Historia Rerum* of **Aeneas Sylvius** (Pius II) and **Pierre d'Ailly**'s *Imago Mundi.*

Ref. *AOS*1 I, 53-54.

GULF OF PARÍA
See **PARÍA, GULF OF.**

GUTIÉRREZ, PEDRO DE (d. ca. 1492)

One of the **ship**'s company of the *Santa María* on CC's **First Voyage,** designated in the crew list as "butler of the king's dais." Morison interprets this to mean that he was a gentleman volunteer rather than a career seaman. CC used him as a messenger to the **cacique Guacanagarí** at the time of the shipwreck of the *Santa María;* he was also among those left to man the fort of **Navidad** when the *Niña* departed. According to **Bartolomé de Las Casas,** Gutiérrez and **Rodrigo de Escobedo** led a gang of Spaniards who toured the island raping and stealing, and thus precipitated the massacre of the garrison at Navidad.

Ref. *AOS*1 I, 188-90, 390; *AOS*2, 146, 224, 302-6, 427.

H

HAITI

The name now given to the republic that occupies the western end of the island in the **West Indies** which CC named La Española (latinized to **Hispaniola**). The name "Haiti," of native origin, was in CC's day given sometimes to the western end of the island and sometimes to the whole island, which today includes both the republic of Haiti and the **Dominican Republic.**

HAITIEN, CAPE

A cape on a rocky peninsula on the north shore of **Haiti.** It encloses a bay on whose eastern shore CC built the colony of **Navidad** from the timbers of the *Santa María*, which was wrecked near the cape on 24 December 1492 during CC's **First Voyage.**

Ref. *AOS1* I, 394; *AOS2*, 297, 305, 426-28.

HAMMOCK

A woven, suspended sling used for sleeping by the native peoples in the **Bahamas** and the **West Indies** when CC arrived. CC first reported them in his *Journal of the First Voyage* in the entry for 17 October 1492. A landing party found them on an island that Morison identifies as **Long Island** in the Bahamas.

Ref. *AOS1* I, 322.

HARANA, BEATRIZ ENRÍQUEZ DE
See **ENRÍQUEZ DE HARANA, BEATRIZ.**

HARANA, DIEGO DE (d. ca. 1492)

A Córdovan cousin of CC's mistress **Beatriz Enríquez de Harana.** Diego enlisted for the **First Voyage** as "marshall of the fleet" and was charged with enforcing punishment against offenders among the crew of the *Santa María* on which he sailed. When the colony of **Navidad** was established after the wreck of the *Santa María,* Diego de Harana was placed in command of the roughly forty men who were left as the first Spanish colonists in the **New World.** He perished with the others before CC returned on the **Second Voyage.**

Ref. *AOS1* I, 112, 187-90, 373-94, II, 95; *AOS2*, 146, 288, 302, 306, 427.

HENRY VII (1457-1509)

King of **England** (1485-1509). After the failure to sell his **Enterprise of the Indies** to King **John II** of **Portugal** in 1484, CC seems to have commissioned his brother **Bartholo-**

mew **Columbus** to present the plan to Henry VII while he himself went to **Spain** to seek the sponsorship of **Ferdinand** and **Isabel.** Bartholomew presented the plan, though the exact year of the presentation is uncertain. Like John II, Henry VII refused to sponsor the plan.

Ref. *AOS*1 I, 119, 140; *AOS*2, 91, 106.

HENRY THE NAVIGATOR (1394-1460) Prince of **Portugal,** of the House of Avis; uncle of **Afonso V,** who held the Portuguese throne when CC arrived in **Lisbon** in 1476; and great-uncle of **John II,** Afonso's son, who held the throne in 1484 and granted CC an audience to propose his **Enterprise of the Indies** (unsuccessfully). Prince Henry the Navigator was responsible for the long-enduring policy of maritime expansion and of searching for a route to the **East Indies** that dominated Portuguese history in the fifteenth century. He, therefore, can be credited with the Portuguese expansion into India and Indian Ocean in the fifteenth and sixteenth centuries.

Ref. *AOS*2, 28-30, 373; *Encyclopedia Britannica,* 11th. ed., s.v. "Henry of Portugal."

HERALDRY
As a knight, viceroy, and admiral, CC was granted the right to bear arms on 20 May 1493. The accompanying coat of arms (in purple, green, and gold) bore, on the upper left, a castle for **Castile;** on the upper right, a lion for León; on the lower left, a representation of islands; and, on the lower right, anchors.

Ref. *AOS*1 II, 16-18.

HERMANDAD, SANTA
See **SANTA HERMANDAD.**

HISPANIOLA
The latinized form of La **Española,** the name CC gave to the island in the **West Indies** that now comprises the territory of the republic of **Haiti** and the **Dominican Republic.** This island, discovered on the **First Voyage,** includes the sites of the first and second Spanish settlements in the **New World, Navidad** and **Isabela.** It also includes the oldest European city in the western hemisphere, **Santo Domingo,** which became CC's capital as **Viceroy of the Indies** and was the staging point for the Spanish conquest of the lands bordering the Caribbean, including Mexico.

HISTORIA RERUM
Historia Rerum Ubique Gestarum, a world history written about 1440 by **Aeneas Sylvius,** pseudonym of Enea Silvio Piccolomini, Pope Pius II. CC owned a copy of the 1477 edition and filled the margins with notes. *See* **POSTILS.**

HISTORIE
A convenient title for the biography of CC written by his son **Ferdinand Columbus,** which survives only in

an Italian translation by Alfonso Ulloa, published in Venice in 1571, entitled *Le historie della vita e dei fatti di Cristoforo Colombo.* This biography was long subject to attacks on its authenticity beginning with the nineteenth-century scholar Henry Harrisse. *Historie* is now generally accepted, however, as a useful source of much authentic information about CC in spite of Ferdinand's attempt to cover up some aspects of his humble origins.

Ref. Ferdinand Columbus, *Le historie della vita e dei fatti di Cristoforo Colombo,* 2 vols., ed. Rinaldo Caddeo (Milan: Alpes, 1930); Ferdinand Columbus, *The Life of the Admiral Christopher Columbus,* ed. and trans. Benjamin Keen (New Brunswick: Rutgers University Press, 1959). English translation of *Historie;* Antonio Rumeu de Armas, *Hernando Colón, historiador del descubrimiento de América* (Madrid: Instituto de Cultura Hispánica, 1973).

HOJEDA, ALONSO DE (ca. 1473-ca. 1540)
A vigorous, high-tempered and talented Andalusian soldier and mariner who accompanied CC on the **Second Voyage** and served as one of his most aggressive leaders in the initial exploration and conquest of **Hispaniola.** He was largely responsible for the Spanish mistreatment of the native peoples which occurred during this exploration. His Machiavellian skill in dealing with the native peoples is demonstrated in his treacherous capture, on CC's behalf, of the most formidable of the **caciques, Caonabó.** Later, in 1498, Hojeda was authorized by **Juan Rodriguez de Fonseca** (without CC's consent) to captain a voyage of discovery on a ship bearing both **Amerigo Vespucci** and **Juan de La Cosa.** On this journey Hojeda visited the Venezuelan coast and exploited the pearl fisheries. Arriving at Hispaniola, he quarreled with **Roldán,** who attempted to capture him and deliver him to CC and viewed him as a privateer intruding into the admiral's preserve. Hojeda evaded capture, sailed to the **Bahamas,** took on a load of enslaved **Lucayan** people, and returned safely to **Spain.** Later he was active in the exploration and colonization of the Colombian coast.

Ref. *AOS1* II, 102-14, 164-72 *passim; AOS2,* 396, 432-34, 443-44, 483, 488-90, 546, 558, 568; *EDA2,* 118-21, 185-94 *passim;* Kirkpatrick Sale, *The Conquest of Paradise: Christopher Columbus and the Columbian Legacy* (New York: Knopf, 1990), 146, 174, 185, 397*n.*4.

HONDURAS
The Central American country whose territory was discovered by CC in early August 1502 on the **Fourth Voyage.** Sailing southwest, against

the **trade winds,** CC took about seven weeks to reach Cape Gracias a Dios, where the coast turns southward and where he was now able to proceed along the north-south coastline of what is now Nicaragua.

Ref. *AOS1* II, 331-39; *AOS2*, 595-601.

HORSE LATITUDES

Mariners' name for an area of high pressure in the Atlantic, north of the belt of **trade winds,** about thirty to thirty-four degrees North **latitude.** Here the sea is frequently very rough. It was in this stretch of water in August 1492 that the *Pinta*'s rudder jumped its gudgeons, requiring the **ship** to put in for repairs at the island of **Grand Canary.**

Ref. *AOS1* I, 265-66; *Encyclopedia Britannica,* 11th ed., s.v. "Horse Latitudes."

HUELVA

A town in southwestern **Spain** on the **Odiel River,** near the river's junction with the **Tinto,** the locale of the **Palos de la Frontera** and the friary of **La Rábida.** CC's sister-in-law Violante (or Briolante) **Molyart,** lived in Huelva, and some scholars conjecture that CC left his son **Diego** in the charge of the Molyart family during part or all of the time the child was being schooled by the Franciscans at La Rábida.

Ref. *AOS1* I, 107-9, 133; *AOS2*, 79-81.

HURRICANES

The extremely violent circular tropical **storms** prevalent in the **West Indies** between June and November. CC had several encounters with hurricanes. Some mariners feel that the heavy swell, under blue skies, that CC encountered mid-Atlantic on the westward voyage in 1492 was caused by a hurricane that was east of CC. A hurricane struck **Isabela** in June 1495 and sank several of **CC's ships** and, in 1502, CC was close enough to **Santo Domingo** on the **Fourth Voyage** to send a message about a forthcoming storm to the governor, **Ovando.** Ovando ignored the message and sent out a fleet of thirty vessels carrying, among many others, **Francisco de Bobadilla,** the cacique **Guarionex,** and CC's former lieutenant **Antonio de Torres.** All three drowned. Nineteen ships went down with all hands and an enormous treasure of **gold** was lost, so much so that CC's share would have made him one of the wealthiest private citizens in Europe. The only surviving ship was the *Aguja,* carrying 4000 pesos in gold consigned to CC; this actually reached **Diego Columbus** and became part of CC's considerable estate. CC's own ships took shelter and rode out the storm.

Ref. *AOS1* II, 172-73, 324-27, 416; *AOS2*, 478-79, 490-91, 590-92.

I

IBERIAN PENINSULA

Standard term for the large peninsula at the southwest corner of Europe which circumscribes **Spain** and **Portugal.**

ICELAND

Ferdinand Columbus writes, in the *Historie*, that CC sailed 100 leagues north of Iceland in February 1477, that the sea was not frozen there, and that the tides in Iceland were fifty feet high. It is entirely possible that CC made such a voyage, but, if so, the fifty-foot tides were witnessed at **Bristol, England,** a normal port of call on such a voyage. That the seas were open that far north in that year has been argued by a Scandinavian scholar, Vilhjamur Stefanson. Indeed there is every reason to believe that the seas would have been open because of the Gulf Stream, though perhaps cluttered with icebergs.

Ref. *EDA2*, 14-15; Ferdinand Columbus, *The Life of the Admiral Christopher Columbus,* ed. and trans. Benjamin Keen (New Brunswick: Rutgers University Press, 1959), chap. 4 *passim;* Vilhjamur Stefanson, *Ultima Thule: Further*

Mysteries of the Arctic (New York: Macmillan, 1940).

IMAGO MUNDI

CC owned a copy of this book by **Pierre d'Ailly** that is now in the **Biblioteca Colombina** in **Seville.** *Imago Mundi* was published in Louvain, in three volumes, from 1480 to 1483. The annotations by CC in the margins are among the most valuable documents for the study of his life. There are, for example, references to his voyage to the **Guinea** coast in the early 1480s, to exploratory voyages made by Portuguese mariners in the Atlantic west of **Portugal,** and to many ideas related to the geography of eastern Asia.

Ref. *AOS1* I, 53-55, 120-25; *AOS2*, 41, 92-95, 557; *EDA2*, 27, 39; Edmund Buron, ed., *Imago Mundi de Pierre d'Ailly* (Paris: Maisonnueve, 1930).

INDIA

A **caravel** of perhaps fifty tons built in **Hispaniola** by CC's shipwrights in 1495/96. Its nickname *India,* was commonly used instead of the name given on commissioning, *Santa Cruz.* In the period from 10 March to 11

June 1496, the *India* and CC's favorite **ship,** the *Niña*, the latter carrying CC, returned to **Spain** to end the **Second Voyage.** The *India,* like the *Niña,* returned to the **West Indies** as part of the fleet on CC's **Third Voyage.**

> Ref. *AOS*1 II, 173-91, 227-28; *AOS*2, 491-500, 511-12; José María Martínez-Hidalgo, "Las naves de los cuatro viajes de Colón al nuevo mundo," *Temi Colombiani* (Genoa: ECIG, 1986), 201-29.

INDIANS

The general name CC gave to the native Americans, which has survived despite attempts to correct CC's false assumption that he had landed in the **Indies.**

INDIES

In the view of many scholars, CC thought to the end of his life that he had discovered the islands, known to Europeans as the Indies, which were the source of the spices the Europeans for centuries had purchased via Arab traders. The Portuguese royal House of Avis had been attempting to reach them throughout the fifteenth century by finding a route around Africa. In his **Enterprise of the Indies,** in fact, CC hoped to reach the Indies by sailing west. It was therefore natural for CC to assume that the persons he found in the **Bahamas** and the **West Indies** were "Indians," and he gave them this name in his *Journal of the First Voyage.* Geography and history were so vague on Asia that CC was convinced at the time of the **Second Voyage** that **Cuba** was the Asiatic mainland, probably a part of Cathay, ruled by the **Grand Khan** whose dynasty in China had, in fact, ended many years before CC's birth.

CC's geographical ideas of the Indies were a hodgepodge; those who believe that his **postils** were written before he sailed on the **First Voyage** ascribe these ideas to *The Book of Ser Marco Polo* and to other late medieval books such as **Pierre d'Ailly's** *Imago Mundi*, and the *Historia Rerum* of **Aeneas Sylvius** (Pius II). CC's personally annotated copies of both books survive. *See* EAST INDIES.

> Ref. Kirkpatrick Sale, *The Conquest of Paradise* (New York: Knopf, 1990), chap. 9 *passim,* contains an analysis of CC's views at the end of his life.

INDIES, ARCHIVE OF THE
See ARCHIVE OF THE INDIES.

INDIES, ENTERPRISE OF THE
See ENTERPRISE OF THE INDIES.

INTER CAETERA
See PAPAL BULLS and DEMARCATION, LINE OF.

IRELAND
In one of his marginal notes in his copy of *Historia Rerum*, CC said he

had visited the port of **Galway** on the Irish western coast. This corroborates **Ferdinand Columbus**'s assertion in his biography of CC—that his father claimed to have sailed to **Iceland** in 1477—since Galway was a regular port of call on the route.

Ref. *AOS*1 I, 32-33; *AOS*2, 24-26; Ferdinand Columbus, *The Life of the Admiral Christopher Columbus,* ed. and trans. Benjamin Keen (New Brunswick: Rutgers University Press, 1959), chap. 4 *passim.*

IRISH

In spite of the persistent myths that one or more Irishmen sailed with CC on his **First Voyage,** the records of the crews of **CC's ships** include no one who can be identified as a native of **Ireland.**

Ref. Alicia Bache Gould, *Nueva Lista Documenta de los Tripulantes de Colón en 1492,* ed. José M. de la Pina (Madrid: Real Academia de la Historia, 1984).

ISABEL I (1451-1504)

Spanish queen of **Castile** and Léon (1474-1504); first queen of a united **Spain,** which she ruled jointly with **Ferdinand V** of **Aragon,** from 1479 to 1504; together they were known as the **Catholic Monarchs.** Isabel was a gifted and forceful ruler whose sympathy with CC's **Enterprise of the Indies** was undoubtedly a major factor in the monarchs' decision to ac-cept the project. Inheriting a monarchy weakened by the vacillation and incompetence of her predecessors, she moved rapidly with Ferdinand to curb the power of the nobles and to solidify the power of the throne, a trend of European monarchs since Philip the Fair of France had begun the movement to make kingship absolute. Isabel was highly respected for her integrity and vigor. Deeply, sometimes fanatically, religious, she wished to draw all her subjects into the Roman Catholic Church and was party to the expulsion in 1492 of all **Jews** who refused to be converted, as well as the 1493 coerced baptism of all **Moors** who remained on the **Iberian Peninsula** after the fall of **Granada. Bartolomé de Las Casas** concluded accurately that Isabel was more sympathetic toward CC and his Enterprise than was Ferdinand. It therefore seems likely that her death was responsible for the increasing isolation from the monarchy that CC experienced after his return from the **Fourth Voyage** in 1504, until his death in 1506. *See* CAPITULATIONS OF **1492** and CATHOLIC MONARCHS.

Ref. R.B. Merriman, *The Rise of the Spanish Empire in the Old World and the New,* vols. 1 and 2 (New York: Macmillan, 1936); Lee Anne Durham Seminario, *The History of the Blacks, the Jews and the Moors in Spain* (Madrid: Playors, S.A., 1975).

ISABELA, TOWN OF

The second Spanish settlement in **Hispaniola,** on the north coast of what is now the Republic of **Haiti,** near the border with the present **Dominican Republic.** The unhealthy and unstrategic site was chosen in haste after CC's fleet of the **Second Voyage,** having just discovered the destruction of **Navidad** and the massacre of its colonists, was unable to make much headway eastward against the **trade winds.** The story of Isabela's construction and its history as the administrative seat of CC's government is one of disease, death, and disillusionment. CC, partly through **Hojeda**'s and others' cruel and aggressive treatment of the native peoples, lost their confidence as well as the support of his colonists. The reports of the poor conditions spread throughout **Spain** with the return of many disgruntled settlers. CC finally felt it necessary to return himself in 1496 to defend his position. In CC's absence, **Bartholomew Columbus,** left in charge, began the construction of **Santo Domingo** on the southern coast, at the mouth of the **Ozama River,** and moved the capital there.

Ref. *AOS*1 II, 96-117, 171-77, 295; *AOS*2, 427-42, 479, 494-95.

ISABELA ISLAND

The name that CC gave to the island in the **Bahamas** that he discovered on 19 October 1492 during the **First Voyage.** The native peoples of **Guanahani** on board **CC's ship** called the island Samoete.

Ref. *AOS*1 I, 324-28; *JOD,* 75-81.

J

JAINA RIVER

A river emptying into **Santo Domingo** Bay, **Hispaniola.** CC landed here during the **Second Voyage** in the *Niña* in late summer 1494 after exploring the southern coast of **Cuba,** discovering **Jamaica** and exploring the southern coast of Hispaniola. He put ashore here to leave a party of nine men assigned to cross the island to **Isabela** with the news that the exploring fleet was safe and would soon return.

Ref. *AOS*1 II, 157, 326.

JAMAICA

An island south of **Cuba** and southwest of **Hispaniola,** discovered by CC on 5 May 1494 prior to his exploration of the southern coast of Cuba during the **Second Voyage.** CC was enthusiastic about its beauty and noted a dense native population (**Tainos,** speaking an Arawak language) and the extensive use of **canoes.** CC's first stop was at a bay that he named Santa Gloria (modern **St. Ann's Bay**), where, in 1504, he and his crews were stranded for more than a year with the remains of two of the **ships** in the fleet of the **Fourth Voyage.**

In 1494 CC sailed from Santa Gloria on to **Montego Bay,** then continued on to Cuba. Near the end of July, CC returned and explored the western and southern shores of Jamaica and part of the eastern shore as far north as Morant Point. From here he sailed back to Hispaniola.

Ref. *AOS*1 II, 117-57; Cecil Jane, ed. and trans., *Select Documents Illustrating the Four Voyages of Columbus,* vol. 1 (London: Hakluyt Society Publications, 1930), 114-67, an extract from *Historia de los Reyes Católicos* by Andrés Bernáldez, printed with English translation.

JAPAN

Under the name Cipangu, used by **Marco Polo,** this was the proposed first destination of CC's **Enterprise of the Indies.** Marco Polo, whose book of travels CC had at least heard of, had placed Japan 1500 miles east of the Chinese coast, making it a logical stopping place on the way to the realm of the **Grand Khan** and the **Indies.** At various points CC identified both **Cuba** and **Hispaniola** with Cipangu.

Ref. *AOS2*, 33-34, 65-68, 137-38, 237-53, 296, 347.

JARDIN DE LA REINA
See QUEEN'S GARDEN.

JERUSALEM
Heavily influenced by the spirit of the Crusades, still strong both in **Genoa** and in **Spain,** CC seriously hoped that the **gold** and other wealth he would find in the **Indies** could finance a crusade by the **Catholic Monarchs** to recover Jerusalem for Christendom. CC's interest in acquiring wealth should be viewed—at least in part—in the context of this idealistic ambition, perhaps a fundamental motive for the **Enterprise of the Indies.**

Ref. Leonard I. Sweet, "Christopher Columbus and the Millennial Vision of the New World," *Catholic Historical Review* 72 (1986): 369-82, 715-16; Pauline Moffitt Watts, "Prophecy and Discovery: On the Spiritual Origins of Christopher Columbus' 'Enterprise of the Indies'," *American Historical Review* 90 (1985): 73-102.

JEWS
Jews and Christians of Jewish extraction, known as "**conversos,**" were a very important element in the life of **Spain** at the time of CC's arrival. The administration of the **Catholic Monarchs** was heavily dependent on members of the converso community. CC frequently met and was aided by influential conversos as he rose to the position of commander of a fleet of exploration. Some scholars, in fact, most notably Salvador de Madariaga, have concluded that CC's well-known skill in bargaining and his habitual insistence on *quid pro quo* are evidence that he himself came from a family of conversos. While the nature of such evidence may well be questioned, this scholarly debate continues. Like almost any other European of his time, CC might have had Jewish ancestors. If so, we do not know who they were; we do know that his mother and father were descended on both sides from Ligurian families who had been Roman Catholic for as far back as they can be traced.

Ref. *AOS1* I, 22-23, 273; *AOS2*, 7, 104, 109, 149, 154, 206; Lee Anne Durham Seminario, *The History of the Blacks, the Jews and the Moors in Spain* (Madrid: Playor, S.A., 1975); Salvador de Madariaga, *Christopher Columbus* (New York: Oxford University Press, 1939), 90-93, 100, 114, 165, 184; Henry Vignaud, "Columbus a Spaniard and a Jew?" *American Historical Review* 18 (1913): 505-12.

JICAQUE INDIANS
Were also known by the Spaniards as Payas. This is the name used to refer to those people living in modern-day Honduras, reportedly a Honduran

kingdom of Maya, when CC arrived along the Honduran land to take possession.

Ref. *AOS2*, 594-600.

JOHN II (1455-1495)

King of Portugal (1481-1495). John was the Portuguese king to whom CC presented his **Enterprise of the Indies** in 1484. John and his family (the House of Avis) had been trying to reach the **Indies,** or the **East Indies** as they were later known, by sea for four generations. John received CC courteously and sought the advice of his geographers, who rejected the idea of sailing west to the Indies as impracticable. In 1488, when the fleet of **Bartholomew Dias,** dispatched to sail around Africa to India, had been gone a very long time, King John wrote to CC in **Spain** and invited him to **Lisbon** for further talks. CC seems to have gone; one marginal note in his copy of **Pierre d'Ailly's** *Imago Mundi* seems to indicate that, at Christmastime in 1488, CC was in Lisbon when Dias returned with the news that his fleet had rounded the south end of Africa, opening the way for a voyage to India. Though it is not clear whether John was considering CC's Enterprise at the time, nothing further came of John's interest in CC. The king had the humiliation in March of 1493 of being visited by CC when the latter was driven by a **storm** into the port of Lisbon on his return from the **First**

Voyage; CC, at the time, appeared to have sailed to the Indies.

Ref. *AOS1* I, 52-53, 97-99, 435-44; *AOS2*, 69-77, 340-49, 367-73.

JOURNAL OF THE FIRST VOYAGE

The *Diario,* diary or daily record kept by CC on the **First Voyage.** It is the first known example of a detailed log of daily occurrences on board ship during a voyage. The only known surviving record of this log is the abstract made by **Bartolomé de Las Casas,** first published by Martín Fernández de Navarrete in 1825.

In the absence of the complete log, the abstract is referred to as the *Journal* or *Diario* as if it were complete. This is not entirely wishful thinking, for Las Casas's abstract, though it undoubtedly abbreviates many things recorded by CC, appears to be quite faithful to CC's intent. The *Journal* probably constitutes a responsible summary of the original and principal historical document recording the first voyage of discovery, and CC's exact words wherever these are essential.

Although the *Journal* was written chiefly for the **Catholic Monarchs** and heavily slanted according to the impression CC wished to make, it constitutes an ineffably rich and detailed account of the voyage of discovery.

Ref. *JOD,* 37-179, an English translation of the *Journal* and extensive commentary; Martín Fernández de Navarette, *Colección de los viages y descubrimientos que hicieron por mar los españoles desde fines del siglo xv, con varios documentos inéditos concernientes á la historia de la marina castellana y de los establecimientos españoles en Indias, coórdinada é ilustrada por don Martin Fernandez de Navarette,* vol. 1 (Madrid: Imprenta real, 1825-37), 1-166.

JUAN, INFANTE DON (1478-1497)

Prince of **Spain;** son of **Isabel** and **Ferdinand,** heir to the thrones of **Castile** and **Aragón** until his death. CC was a close friend of Doña **Juana de Torres,** who had been governess to the prince, a connection probably based on the fact that **Diego** and **Ferdinand Columbus,** while in training to be pages to the sovereigns, were schooled at court with the prince. When CC was returned in chains from **Hispaniola** in October 1500 at the end of the **Third Voyage,** he wrote a letter to Doña Juana that detailed his conflict with the settlers in Hispaniola and with **Francisco de Bobadilla.** This important letter, which CC knew would be communicated to the sovereigns, is a chief source of our knowledge of CC's position at this time and undoubtedly led the sovereigns to force Bobadilla to give back much of the personal property that he had taken from CC in Hispaniola.

Ref. *AOS2,* 508-9, 555; *JOD,* 289-302.

K

KHAN, GRAND

The title used by **Marco Polo** for the Emperor of China, a member of the Mongol dynasty (officially called the Yüan dynasty). Since Polo's time, Turkish domination in the eastern Mediterranean had completely cut off China from western Europe. Therefore, neither CC nor his contemporaries knew that the title of Khan and the Mongol dynasty had ceased to exist in 1368. CC expected to encounter the domains and subjects of the Grand Khan and carried letters of introduction from the **Catholic Monarchs** intended for the Khan and other Far Eastern potentates. CC searched for cities and representatives of the Khan when he discovered **Cuba** in October 1492. When apprised of the **Caribs,** or cannibals, by the natives he had captured on Guanahani, he associated *cannibal* with *Khan* and assumed that the Caribs lived on a continent south of Cuba and **Hispaniola.**

Ref. *AOS*1 I, 45-46, 124, 140-42, 187, 203, 359, 370; *AOS*2, 107-8, 150, 257-58, 274, 283; Alicia Bache Gould, ''Nueva lista documentada de los tripulantes de Colón en 1492,'' *Boletin de la Real Academia de la Historia* (Madrid) 90 (1927): 544-45; Henry Vignaud, *Historie critique de la grande entreprise de Christophe Colomb,* vol. 2 (Paris: Welter, 1911), 582; Kirkpatrick Sale, *The Conquest of Paradise: Christopher Columbus and the Columbian Legacy* (New York: Knopf, 1990), 25, 26, 64, 65, 94, 108, 109, 119, 127, 175, 209, 375-76*n*.6.

L

LA COSA, JUAN DE (ca. 1460-1509)
The owner of the *Santa María*, flagship of the **First Voyage.** According to CC's *Journal of the First Voyage*, La Cosa disobeyed CC's orders when the **ship** went aground on the north shore of **Hispaniola** on 24 December 1492, abandoning the ship when he was needed to help pull it off the reef.

The name Juan de La Cosa appears three more times: a crew member in the *Niña* on the **Second Voyage;** a man who made a voyage to the Caribbean in 1499 with **Alonso de Hojeda** and **Amerigo Vespucci;** and one who made a widely circulated world map dated 1500, but frequently assigned to 1510 or thereabouts. It has been a matter of dispute whether these were one, two, or three men. *See* CUBA.

Ref. *AOS1* I, 186-98, 386-90; *AOS2*, 144-45, 300-02, 466-67; Roberto Barreiro Meiro, "Algo sobre la carta de Juan de la Cosa," *Revista General de Marina* (Madrid) 183 (1972): 3-8; Roberto Barreiro Meiro, "Juan de la Cosa y su doble personalidad," *Revista General de Marina* (Madrid) 179 (1970): 165-91; Arthur Davies, "The Date of Juan de la Cosa's World Map and its Implication for American Discovery," *Geographical Journal* (London) 142 (1976): 111-16; Fernando Royo Guardia, "Don Cristóbal Colón, la insularidad de Cuba, y el mapa de Juan de la Cosa," *Revista de Indias* (Madrid) 28 (1968): 433-73.

LAGOS
A town on the southern coast of **Portugal** just east of **Cape St. Vincent,** the promontory at the southwest corner of the **Iberian Peninsula.** In August 1476, CC may have been on board the Flemish ship *Bechalla* in a Genoese convoy headed for Ghent in the Low Countries when the convoy was attacked by French pirates led by **Guillaume de Casenove.** The *Bechalla* was sunk, and some historians believe that CC survived by clinging to a broken oar, swimming to shore near Lagos. If so, this was the beginning of CC's nine-year association with Portugal.

LA MINA
See MINA, SAN JORGE DA.

LANDFALL

The term for sighting and arriving at land, whether island or mainland, at the end of a leg of a voyage. In CC studies, the term usually refers to the arrival of the fleet of the **First Voyage** at the island of **Guanahani** on 12 October 1492.

LANDFALL QUESTION

One of the most controversial and longest-lived issues in CC scholarship is the question of which island in the **Bahamas** is to be identified as **Guanahani,** the island where CC landed on 12 October 1492. Currently, **San Salvador Island** (also called Watlings Island; CC called Guanahani "San Salvador"), **Grand Turk,** and **Samana Cay,** are thought to be among the most likely, although many other islands have been proposed.

Ref. Joseph Judge, "Where Columbus Found the New World," *National Geographic* 170 (November 1986): 566-99; John Parker, "The Columbus Landfall Problem: A Historical Perspective," *Terrae Incognitae* 15 (1983): 1-28.

LANZAROTE ISLAND

The easternmost of the **Canary Islands,** controlled in CC's day by the Peraza family and in 1492 by **Beatriz de Bobadilla y Peraza,** who, after her husband's death in 1487, also controlled Fuerteventura, **Ferro,** and **Gomera.**

Ref. *AOS*1 I, 211; R.B. Merriman, *The Rise of the Spanish Empire in the Old World and the New,* vol. 1 (New York: Macmillan, 1936).

LA RÁBIDA

Santa María de la Rábida, the name of a Franciscan friary located just south of the town of **Palos** in **Spain** on the **Tinto** river. When he arrived in Spain in 1485, CC may have left his son **Diego** at La Rábida for schooling while he sought the support of the **Catholic Monarchs.** This friary was a focal point of CC's activity in Spain when he was seeking the sponsorship of the monarchs for his **Enterprise of the Indies.** Two priests frequently associated with the friary, **Antonio de Marchena** and **Juan Pérez,** helped him to secure aid. Marchena, who could have been resident at La Rábida in 1485, may have aided CC in getting his initial interview with the monarchs on 20 January 1486; and Pérez in 1491 visited Queen **Isabel** at the siege fortress of **Santa Fé** and persuaded her to reopen relations with CC regarding his Enterprise. Although there were still disagreements and difficulties, Juan Pérez's interventions were decisive and, after the fall of **Granada** on 2 January 1492, the negotiations moved forward to a successful conclusion in the **Capitulations of 1492.** CC's center of activity at Palos during the securing and preparation of ships and re-cruiting of the crew appears to have been La Rábida.

Ref. *AOS*1 I, 107-29; Juan Man-zano Manzano, *Cristóbal Colón: Siete Años Decisivos de su Vida, 1485-1492* (Madrid: Ediciones Cultura Hispánica, 1964); Anton-io Rumeu de Armas, *La Rábida y el descubrimiento de América: Colón, Marchena y fray Juan Pérez* (Madrid: Cultura His-pánica, 1968).

LAS CASAS, BARTOLOMÉ DE (1474-1566)

A Spanish missionary to the Ameri-can **Indians.** As a young man, before he became a priest, Las Casas went to **Hispaniola** in 1500 to make his for-tune at the urging of his father and uncle, who had gone there as colo-nists on CC's **Second Voyage** in 1494. Unlike most other Europeans, he was distressed by the mistreatment of the native peoples and decided to dedi-cate his life to improving their lot. He was ordained a priest in 1510 and, besides campaigning tirelessly to abolish Indian **slavery,** engaged in many activities on behalf of the Indi-ans, including an attempt to establish a model colony for them in 1520/21. He became bishop of Chiapas, Mexi-co. Las Casas made long visits to **Spain** attempting to change official policy respecting the native Ameri-cans and, as a result, humanitarian ''New Laws'' were adopted in 1542 which, however, were soon altered and made ineffective.

Las Casas became a close friend of CC and of his son **Diego,** who was second **Viceroy of the Indies.** His scholarly *Historia de las Indias,* writ-ten between 1527 and 1563, provides one of the very best sources of infor-mation on CC, including remarkably balanced and incisive views of his ill treatment of the native population. CC's policies and actions reduced the native population in Hispaniola from approximately 300,000 before 1492 to about 60,000 by 1508. Las Casas's published attack on his countrymen's cruelty and rapacity toward the Indi-ans, the *Apologetica Historia* (1530), was eagerly picked up and translated by Spain's enemies and gave rise to the ''Black Legend,'' a virulent ac-count of Spanish cruelties in the **New World** that tarnished the reputation of Spain. So forcefully did the Span-ish resent Las Casas that his *Historia* was not printed until 1875.

Ref. *AOS*1 I, 70, II, 173-74; *AOS*2, 44-46, 72-73, 87-88, 97-103, 155-56, 172-73, 291, 396, 443, 493-94, 515, 544-45; Bartolomé de Las Casas, *Historia de las Indi-as,* 3 vols., ed. Agustín Millares Carlo (Mexico City and Buenos Aires: Fondo de Cultura Económi-ca, 1951), revised in 1972, with an introduction by Lewis Hanke; Bartolomé de Las Casas, *Popery Truly Display'd in Its Bloody*

Colours; or A Faithful Narrative of the Horrid and Unexampled Massacres, Butcheries, and All Manner of Cruelties, That Hell and Malice Could Invent, Committed by the Popish Spanish Party on the Inhabitants of West-India. . . . (London: R. Hewson, 1689); William S. Maltby, *The Black Legend in England: The Development of Anti-Spanish Sentiment, 1558-1660* (Durham: Duke University Press, 1971).

LAS PALMAS

The capital of the island of **Grand Canary** in the **Canary Islands.** On the **First Voyage,** the *Pinta* and probably the *Niña* underwent repairs at Las Palmas before the fleet proceeded on its route westward across the Atlantic. The *Pinta*'s rudder was repaired and the rigging on one of these **ships** was changed from **lateen** to square. CC may have visited Las Palmas at some time during his Portuguese years, from 1476 to 1485; however, there is no solid evidence that this is more than a local legend.

LATEEN SAIL

A triangular sail supported from the top by a spar affixed to a mast at an acute angle. The sail was imported to the Mediterranean from the Indian Ocean where the Arabs developed it. The Portuguese, in exploring the west coast of Africa, found the sail particularly useful for sailing against headwinds; their **caravels,** intended for extensive use along the African coast, bore only lateen sails on their three or four masts. CC's fleet on the **First Voyage** was square-rigged, with a single lateen sail on the rear, or mizzenmast, because CC wished to scud with the **trade winds.**

Ref. *AOS1* I, xxxvii-xli, 153-54, 213-14.

LATITUDE

A term indicating the angular distance of any point on the surface of the earth from the equator. The latitude of the equator is zero degrees, the latitude of the North Pole is ninety degrees North latitude, and the latitude of Cairo, Egypt and of New Orleans is about thirty degrees North latitude.

LATITUDE SAILING

A navigational plan for reaching a specific point across a large body of water, especially an ocean, by first sailing to the **latitude** of the point desired and then crossing the water on that latitude by heading straight east or west, maintaining a particular compass bearing confirmed daily by the bearing at which a certain star rises in the evening. Some students of CC's **navigation** think he employed latitude sailing in crossing the Atlantic, but there is little or no evidence in his *Journal of the First Voyage* or in any of his other writings to verify this. His discovery of the curious shift in compass variation in the course of an Atlantic crossing might well have shaken any belief he might have had that such a plan was reliable.

LEDESMA, PEDRO DE (n.d.)
A pilot on one of **CC's ships** on the **Third Voyage,** taken on board during the fleet's stop at **Funchal, Madeira.** On the **Fourth Voyage,** Ledesma joined the mutiny against CC while the expedition was stranded at **Jamaica.** Later, teaming up with the **Pinzóns,** Ledesma testified against CC in **Los Pleitos,** the suit by **Diego Columbus** against the crown to claim the privileges granted in the **Capitulations of 1492.**

Ref. *AOS1* I, 199, II, 236, 264, 321, 375, 408; *AOS2*, 518, 586, 631, 657.

LEONOR, DONA (1485-1525)
Queen of **Portugal,** wife of **John II,** and sister of John's successor, **Emanuel I.** When CC visited King John at the monastery of **Santa María das Virtudes** in March 1493, after taking refuge in the **Tagus River** from an Atlantic **storm** at the end of his **First Voyage,** he accepted an invitation from Queen Leonor to visit her at the nearby convent of **San Antonio de Castanheira.** The king and queen were at country retreats to escape an infection raging in **Lisbon** at the time. A conflicting story (also reported by Morison) has it that only the queen was at the convent at the time, and gives no mention of escaping an infection.

Ref. *AOS2*, 347-48; *JOD,* 173-78.

LESSER ANTILLES
That part of the **West Indies** that extends south from **Antigua** to **Trinidad.** Called "lesser" because this group includes no islands as large as **Jamaica,** the smallest of the **Greater Antilles.**

LETTER OF CREDENCE
See **CREDENCE, LETTER OF.**

LETTER TO SANTANGEL
The letter of 4 March 1493 dispatched from **Lisbon** by CC to **Luis de Santangel** in **Barcelona,** communicating through Santangel to the **Catholic Monarchs** the first written account of the **First Voyage.** The Letter became one of the most widely published and circulated items of the day, apprising much of Europe of CC's discovery in a very short time. A copy of the Letter was also dispatched by CC to Gabriel Sánchez.

Ref. Cecil Jane, "The Letter of Columbus Announcing the Success of His First Voyage," *Hispanic American Historical Review* 10 (1930): 33-50; Cecil Jane, *Select Documents Illustrating the Four Voyages of Columbus,* vol. I (London: Hakluyt Society Publications, 1930), a text with facing-page translation.

LIGURIA

The region in which **Genoa** is located, along the Mediterranean at the western end of the **Alps,** touching the present-day French border near **Nice.** The scholars of Genoa have assembled compendious information concerning Liguria in CC's time.

Ref. Gaetano Ferro, ed., *La Liguria e Genova al tempo di colombo. Nuova Raccolta Colombiana,* vol. 11 (Rome: Istituto Poligrafico e Zecca dello Stato, 1988), two tomes.

LINE OF DEMARCATION

See DEMARCATION, LINE OF.

LISBON

The city on the **Tagus River,** capital of **Portugal,** whose maritime activity was a probable inspiration for CC's **Enterprise of the Indies.** CC came here in 1476, possibly after being shipwrecked during a sea fight between a Genoese convoy and French corsairs led by **Guillaume de Casenove.** Employed in Lisbon as a seagoing commercial agent by the Genoese firm of **di Negro,** CC may have met his wife **Felipa Perestrello e Moniz** in the city. The family of Felipa's mother, Isabel Moniz, was one of the most prominent in Portugal, and this connection may have paved the way for CC's audience in 1484 with **John II** in which the mariner offered the Enterprise of the Indies to Portugal and was refused. CC left Portugal around 1485 after the death of his wife, but returned around 1488 at the invitation of John II, perhaps to discuss the Enterprise further. His last visit to Portugal occurred in March 1493 when he took refuge from an Atlantic **storm** in the Tagus. On this occasion he visited John II and told him of his discovery; John was apparently vexed, but treated CC courteously and sent him on to **Spain.**

Ref. *AOS*1 I, 38-107, 431-48; *AOS*2, 27, 32, 33, 35-38, 63-76, 340-50; *JOD,* 173-78.

LONG ISLAND

A relatively long, narrow island in the **Bahamas,** west of **San Salvador Island** (also known as Watlings Island), running northwest to southeast. Those who take San Salvador to be the site of CC's 12 October 1492 **landfall** on the **First Voyage** make Long Island the site of CC's second landing on 15 October 1492.

Ref. *AOS*1 I, 316-24; *AOS*2, 239-45; *JOD,* 70-75, *n.* 80-81.

LONGITUDE

The distance in angular degrees east or west of the prime meridian. In CC's day there was no reliable means of measuring longitude at sea, and it remained so until the eighteenth century.

Ref. *AOS*1 I, 242-43.

LOS PLEITOS DE COLÓN

The litigation against the Spanish crown by CC's heirs to claim the rights granted to CC in the **Capitulations**

of 1492. **Diego Columbus** conducted a series of suits against the crown
to determine the value of the entailed
estate created by CC's wills, resulting in judgments in 1511, 1520, and
1525; but the original litigation was
not completed until 1556, long after
Diego was dead. After the direct male
line ended with the death of **Luis
Colón** in 1578, litigation over the
identity of the prime heir resumed
among the descendants until the final
judgement in 1796 when the victori-
ous litigant took over CC's titles. The
current successor bears CC's Spanish
name, Cristóbal Colón. The suits are
important to the study of CC because
many of the persons most directly
associated with CC testified and gave
evidence pertinent to CC's life. Some
of the records of the trials have been
published.

Ref. *AOS1* I, 177-78; *AOS2*, 135-
36; C. Fernández Duro, *Colección
de documentos ineditos ... de
ultramar,* ser. 2, vols. 7 and 8. *De
los pleitos de Colón* (Madrid:
Sucesores de Rivadeneyra, 1892-
94), partial record of the trial; Antonio Muro Orejón, ed., *Pleitos
Colombinos,* vols. 1, 2, 3 and 8
(Seville: Escuela de Estudios
Hispano-Americanos, 1967-), a
critical edition in progress; Otto
Schoenrich, *The Legacy of Columbus: The Historic Litigations
Involving His Discoveries, His Will,
His Family, and His Descendants,*

2 vols. (Glendale, CA: Arthur H.
Clark, 1949-50).

LUCAYAN
The term applied to the **Taino Indians** who lived in the **Bahama Islands** at the time of CC's arrival in
1492. Like the Tainos in **Cuba,
Hispaniola,** and **Puerto Rico,** they
spoke the **Arawak** language.

Ref. Irving Rouse, "Origin and
Development of the Indians Dis-
covered by Columbus," *Proceed-
ings of the First San Salvador
Conference: Columbus and His
World,* comp. Donald T. Gerace
(Ft. Lauderdale: The College Cen-
ter of the Finger Lakes Bahamian
Field Station, 1987), 293-312.

LUCERNA, ABBOT OF (n.d.)
A cosmographer who arrived in **Isabela**
in the summer of 1494. He took issue
with CC's claim that **Cuba** is not an
island.

Ref. *AOS1* II, 141-42; *JOD,* 227,
"Letter on the Second Voyage"
by Michele de Cuneo.

LUNAR ECLIPSE OF 1504
In June 1503, CC had grounded his
two worm-infested **ships, *Capitana***
and ***Santiago*,** at **St. Ann's Bay** on
the northwest shore of **Jamaica** to
avoid sinking at sea. By the following February the native peoples, by
then completely disillusioned by the
Spaniards' oppression, refused to
give any more food or other supplies
to the Spanish, who still waited for

aid from **Hispaniola.** CC, noticing in his copy of the **Regiomontanus** almanac *Ephemerides* that a lunar eclipse was due on the night of 29 February 1504, summoned the leaders of the natives to a conference about sunset and told them that God would inflict disasters on them if they did not supply the Spaniards, and that God would second this warning with a mighty sign by darkening the moon as it rose. When the moon rose in eclipse, the terrified Indians promptly agreed to supply the Spaniards. After this, the Spaniards were accorded supplies until their rescue in June 1504.

Ref. *AOS*1 II, 401-3; *AOS*2, 654-55; *JOD,* 361-62; English translation of Ferdinand Columbus's account (*Historie,* chap. 103).

LUXAN, JUAN DE (n.d.)
A member of CC's expedition that set out 12 March 1494 to explore territory south of **Isabela** in **Hispaniola.** After CC's expedition climbed the central range and founded the Fort of **Santo Tomás,** Luxan was sent south into the mountains and returned reporting that he had found **gold.**

Ref. *AOS*1 II, 112, 115.

M

MADEIRA

An archipelago on the Atlantic Ocean off Morocco. Known to the Romans, the islands were rediscovered and occupied by **Portugal** in the fifteenth century. The largest island, Madeira, was the center of a flourishing sugar trade (based on the local cane crop) at the time CC arrived in **Lisbon** in 1476. CC was in Madeira on business in 1478.

From about 1479 to 1482, CC probably resided both in **Funchal** and on the other inhabited island of the archipelago, **Porto Santo,** with his wife **Felipa Perestrello e Moniz,** whom CC married around 1479. Porto Santo was under the control of Felipa's brother, Bartholomew Perestrello. CC's father-in-law, also named Bartholomew Perestrello, had occupied the island and settled it for the Portuguese crown and was awarded the captaincy of the island. It seems likely that CC's voyages to the Portuguese-controlled African coast, including the **gold**-mining and **slave**-trading center of **La Mina,** occurred during the time he lived in the Madeira Islands. CC stopped at Funchal on 10 June 1498 for supplies at the outset of the **Third Voyage.** He seems to have had a warm reception from friends there. He also took on a pilot, **Pedro de Ledesma,** who, on the **Fourth Voyage,** joined the mutiny against CC and later testified against CC's heirs in **Los Pleitos.** *See As-SERETO DOCUMENT.*

Ref. *AOS1* I, 41-51, II, 235-36; *AOS2,* 29, 371-74, 517-18; A. Teixeira da Mota, "Colón y los Portugueses," *El viaje de Diogo de Teive. Colón y los Portugueses,* Cuadernos Colombinos no. 5 (Valladolid: Casa-Museo de Colón, 1975), 30-63.

MAGELLAN, FERDINAND (ca. 1480-1521)

In Portuguese, Fernão de Magalhaes, a Portuguese navigator. He fulfilled CC's ambition of reaching the **Spice Islands** by sailing west; his crew was the first to circumnavigate the globe. Magellan's voyage led to the distinction between the **West** and **East Indies,** until that time thought to be one group of islands.

Magellan, born in Sabrosa or Nobrega, served the Portuguese as a mariner in expeditions to the East

Indies but left Portuguese service when he fell out with the crown. He proposed to the Spanish crown his project of reaching the Pacific Spice Islands, known as the **Moluccas,** by sailing west. The project was accepted, and Magellan sailed in 1519 as commander of five ships. After a turbulent winter in Patagonia that included mutiny and the return to **Spain** of one of the ships, Magellan passed through the strait that today bears his name and north along the Pacific coast of South **America** to pick up the **trade winds** which blew the fleet across the Pacific to the Philippines. Magellan was killed in a skirmish with the Filipinos, but one of the ships, the *Victoria*, completed the voyage around the world, arriving in **Cádiz** in 1521.

The voyage is recounted in the exciting first-hand report of the Italian Antonio Pigafetta.

Magellan's voyage brought the Spanish and Portuguese empires into collision, an eventuality that Pope **Alexander VI** had temporarily delayed by the **papal bulls** of 1493 that led to the Treaty of Tordesillas. This treaty had established a north-south line in the Atlantic between the areas being explored and developed by the two countries.

Ref. *EDA*2, 313-30; Charles E. Nowell, ed., *Magellan's Voyage Around the World: Three Contemporary Accounts* (Evanston: Northwestern University Press, 1962), an excellent collection of sources on Magellan.

MAIZE

From the **Arawak** *mahiz,* meaning "corn." **Indians** cultivated corn in the **Bahamas** and the **West Indies** as they did throughout North and South **America**. CC's reference in his *Journal* entry of 16 October 1492 to cultivated panizo (panic grass) on the second island he visited probably is a reference to maize; if so, it is the first European reference to this crop.

Ref. *AOS*1 I, 319; S.E. Morison, ed. and trans., *Journals and Other Documents on the Life and Voyages of Christopher Columbus* (New York: Heritage, 1963), 72-73.

MANATEE

The Caribbean sea-cow, which at a distance can have a human appearance when emerging from the sea. Manatees were often thought to be mermaids. CC reported seeing three manatees off the north coast of **Hispaniola** in his *Journal* entry of 9 January 1493.

Ref. *AOS*1 I, 397-98; *AOS*2, 309-10; *JOD,* 148.

MANCHINEEL

The manzanillo, a tree that CC's men found on Mariegalante, the island between **Guadeloupe** and **Dominica** that was CC's **landfall** on the **Second Voyage.** The fruit of the manchineel provided the poison into which the **Caribs** dipped their arrows.

Ref. *AOS*1 II, 68-69.

MANDEVILLE, SIR JOHN (ca. 1300-1372)

The reputed author of a medieval travel book full of fantastic stories about strange people and animals in little-known parts of Africa and Asia. CC seems to have drawn on remembered passages in Mandeville in his accounts of the **Caribs** and of other exotic items in his **West Indies** experiences.

Ref. *AOS*1 I, 320, 340, 359, II, 34, 128-29, 133, 292; *AOS*2, 377, 454-58; P.C. Hamelius, ed., *Mandeville's Travels,* 2 vols. (London: Paul, Trench & Trubner, 1919-23), Early English Text Society, Original Series nos. 153, 154.

MANGI

A province in southeastern China as described by **Marco Polo. Paolo Toscanelli,** in a letter to the Portuguese diplomat **Fernão Martins,** suggests to the Portuguese government that the Chinese city of **Quinsay,** capital of Mangi, lies 5000 miles due west of **Lisbon.** Having, it seems, received a copy of this letter, CC, reaching **Cuba,** appears to have thought he had reached Mangi.

Ref. *AOS*1 I, 46-47, II, 133; *AOS*2, 458, 465, 554, 637.

MANICAOTEX (n.d.)

A **cacique** in **Hispaniola** at the time of CC's tribute system or **encomiendas** (1495-96), who was reportedly required to pay "a calabash full of gold valued at 150 castellanos every two months."

Ref. *AOS*2, 491.

MANUEL I (MANOEL I)
See **EMANUEL I.**

MARCHENA, FRAY ANTONIO DE (n.d.)

A Franciscan astronomer who appears to have aided CC when he first arrived in **Spain** in 1485. Marchena was the administrator of the Franciscan sub-province of **Seville.** CC may have met him at **La Rábida** or may have been referred to him; it could have been Marchena who succeeded in getting CC an appointment with the Spanish sovereigns in **Córdova** on 20 January 1486. This meeting led to the formation of a royal commission to assess the **Enterprise of the Indies** and, ultimately, to the royal acceptance of the proposal in 1492. The crown suggested to CC that he take Marchena along as an expert cosmologist on the **Second Voyage,** but there is no evidence that CC tried to comply with this suggestion.

Ref. *AOS*1 I, 108-10; *AOS*2, 80-81, 398; Juan Manzano Manzano, *Cristóbal Colón: siete años decisivos en su vida, 1485-1492* (Madrid: Ediciones Cultura Hispánica, 1964); Antonio Rumeu de Armas,

La Rábida y el descubrimiento de América: Colón, Marchena, y fray Juan Pérez (Madrid: Cultura Hispánica, 1968).

MARCO POLO
See **POLO, MARCO.**

MARGARIT, MOSEN PEDRO (n.d.)
A Spanish military officer who commanded **Santo Tomás,** the first inland fort constructed by CC in **Hispaniola.** The fort was built in March 1494, south of the **Vega Real** in the central mountain range of the island, to control that area. Margarit fell out with CC before the admiral returned to **Spain** in 1496 and returned to Spain himself when CC's governing council tried to control his actions.

Ref. *AOS1* II, 56, 112-14, 165-67; *AOS2*, 396, 441-43, 483-87.

MARGINAL NOTES
See **POSTILS.**

MARÍAGALANTE
The nickname given to the *Santa María* (II), flagship of the **Second Voyage,** which, like the *Santa María* of the **First Voyage,** was a nao, or **carrack,** and not a **caravel.** This second *Santa María* was one of CC's favorite ships; CC named the **landfall** island of the Second Voyage for it—Santa María la Galante. CC kept the *Maríagalante* with him at **Isabela,** along with four other ships, when he sent the bulk of the fleet back to **Spain.** CC returned to Spain aboard

the *Maríagalante* at the end of the Second Voyage in the spring of 1496. *See* **SECOND VOYAGE OF DISCOVERY** and **SHIPS, CC'S.**

Ref. *AOS1* II, 55, 67, 88, 115; *AOS2*, 395, 435, 444; José María Martínez-Hidalgo, "Las naves de los cuatro viajes de Colón al nuevo mundo," *Temi Colombiani* (Genoa: ECIG, 1986), 201-29.

MARINUS OF TYRE (b. ca. A.D. 150)
An early cosmographer from whom CC and his brother **Bartholomew** ascertained that the distance by land from **Portugal** to the eastern tip of Asia was two hundred twenty-five degrees rather than the one hundred eighty degrees indicated by **Ptolemy.** This idea was presumably very influential in persuading CC that the ocean west of Portugal was narrow enough to sail across in a few weeks.

Ref. *AOS1* I, 87-90, 103; *AOS2*, 65, 68.

MÁRQUEZ, DIEGO (n.d.)
A Spaniard from **Seville** who, in November 1493 on the **Second Voyage,** took an exploring and plundering party of ten ashore on the island of **Guadeloupe.** When this party got lost, CC sent a search party of 200 to find them. This second party found evidence of cannibal activity on the island, including a number of **Taino** captives whom the Spaniards took back to the ships along with some of the **Caribs.**

Ref. *AOS*1 II, 69-70; *JOD,* 211-12, "Letter on the Second Voyage" by Michele de Cuneo.

MARTINIQUE

CC's **landfall** on the **Fourth Voyage,** 15 June 1502; presumably the same island as that one called Mantinino by the **Indians.** CC heard of Mantinino from the native peoples on the **First Voyage;** he understood them to say that the island was populated exclusively by women, who allowed men to come ashore only occasionally for amorous, or simply procreative, purposes.

Ref. *AOS*1 I, 404-40, II, 323; *AOS*2, 316, 558-59.

MARTINS, FERNÃO (n.d.)

A Portuguese priest and diplomat acquainted with the Florentine physician and cosmographer **Paolo del Pozzo Toscanelli.** Toscanelli sent Martins a letter and a map describing a course west from **Lisbon** to the city of **Quinsay** in the province of **Mangi,** China, including reference to the island of **Japan.** CC acquired a copy of this letter, perhaps by writing to Toscanelli himself, and used it as evidence that his **Enterprise of the Indies** had modern scientific support. Some important scholars have strongly opposed the idea that Toscanelli ever wrote to CC or that Fernão Martins existed, and have rejected the whole matter as a fabrication, perhaps invented by **Bartolomé de Las Casas, Ferdinand Columbus,** or CC's brother, **Bartholomew Columbus;** but since evidence appeared of Martins's status as a member of the Portuguese diplomatic mission to the Vatican, and with the gradual acknowledgement of Las Casas's probity and Ferdinand's general respectability, the idea that CC might have had a letter from Toscanelli has seemed more plausible. It seems unlikely, in any event, that CC originally got the idea for his Enterprise from Toscanelli, although Toscanelli's approval of and dependence on **Marco Polo** may have given CC more faith in the Venetian traveler's book.

Ref. *AOS*1 I, 45-46, 57, 86; Thomas Goldstein, *Dawn of Modern Science from the Arabs to Leonardo Da Vinci* (Boston: Houghton Mifflin, 1980), 15-29, a concise account of Toscanelli's contributions to the European discovery of America.

MARTYR, PETER (1457-1526)

Petrus Martyr Anglerius. The earliest historian of the **New World,** a term that he coined. Born near Lago Maggiore, Italy, he was educated in the Italian humanist tradition. He went to **Spain** at the age of thirty and became a courtier. He lectured in **Salamanca** and fought in the war against the **Moors.** He was present in **Barcelona** when CC returned from the **First Voyage** in 1493 and decided around 1494 to write a history of the discovery and conquest of the

"Indies," ultimately published as *De Orbe Novo* in eight sections or "decades." The first decade, which contains important information on CC, was published in Venice in 1504. *See* TREVISAN, ANGELO DE.

Ref. *AOS*2, 51-52, 232, 382-84, 471-73; E. Lunardi, E. Magioncalda, and R. Mazzacane, eds., *La scoperta del Nuovo Mondo negli scritti di Pietro Martire d'Anghiera,* vol. 6 (Rome: Nuova Raccolta Colombiana and I.P.Z.S., 1988), a new critical edition; F.A. McNutt, *De Orbe Novo, the Eight Decades of Peter Martyr d'Anghiera* (New York and London: G.P. Putnam, 1912), English translation.

MASTIC

A gummy substance made from the sap of the lentisk tree that flourishes on the island of **Chios** where, in CC's day, a large cash crop of the substance was gathered and sold by the Genoese to European customers who believed in its medicinal qualities. The Genoese convoy of August 1476, carrying mastic to northern Europe, included the *Bechalla,* wrecked off the coast of **Portugal** with CC perhaps on board. When CC was exploring **Cuba** and **Hispaniola** on the **First Voyage** he thought he saw the profitable lentisk tree and reported this to the Spanish sovereigns as evidence of the value of his discovery.

Ref. *AOS*1 I, 30-31.

MEDEL, ALONSO (n.d.)

A mariner of **Palos** who served as master of the *Niña* when CC took the **caravel,** along with the *San Juan* and *Cardera,* to explore the coastline of **Cuba** in April 1494 to determine whether this land was part of the mainland of Asia.

Ref. *AOS*1 II, 117; *AOS*2, 496, 511.

MEDINA SIDONIA, DON ENRIQUE DE GUZMAN (d. 1492)

Second duke of Medina Sidonia. The wealthiest grandee of **Spain** in CC's day, to whom CC may have appealed for aid for his **Enterprise of the Indies.** This might have been shortly after CC arrived in 1485, or in the period 1488/89. There is no documentation other than the assertion in **Ferdinand Columbus**'s and **Las Casas**'s biographies that CC sought the duke's aid.

Ref. *AOS*2, 82.

MEDINACELI, DON LUIS DE LA CERDA (n.d.)

Fifth count of Medinaceli. A wealthy, honorable, and accomplished nobleman who aided CC during his seven-year bid for support of his **Enterprise of the Indies** from the Spanish sovereigns. Medinaceli wrote a letter (intended for the queen) to Cardinal **Mendoza** in which he cited his aid to CC and his recommendation of CC's Enterprise. There is some controversy over when this occurred. Some evidence suggests that this help occurred shortly after CC's arrival in **Spain,** before the mariner had made contact with the queen; but known facts about CC and the monarchs argue that the help (chiefly in the form of providing him with a residence) must have occurred around 1489/90 and that Medinaceli's letter, undated, must have been written after the **First Voyage.**

Ref. *AOS1* I, 115-38, II, 32, 103; *AOS2*, 82, 98, 375, 432; Juan Manzano Manzano, *Cristóbal Colón: siete años decisivos de su vida, 1485-1492* (Madrid: Ediciones Cultura Hispánica, 1964); Antonio Rumeu de Armas, *La Rábida y el descubrimiento de América: Colón, Marchena, y fray Juan Pérez* (Madrid: Cultura Hispánica, 1968), chap. 6 *passim.*

MÉNDEZ, DIEGO (d. 1536)

A gentleman volunteer aboard the *Santiago* on CC's **Fourth Voyage.** Méndez served faithfully on the voyage and intrepidly in battles with **Indians** and rebel crew. Méndez also engineered the rescue of CC and the crews who had been stranded on **Jamaica** for over a year, when he, with **Bartolomeo Fieschi** and two **canoes** rowed by Spaniards and Jamaican Indians, crossed the passage to **Hispaniola** against the **trade winds** and, without support from the governor, **Ovando,** secured a **caravel** in

Santo Domingo and rescued CC and the remaining crew.

Ref. *AOS2*, 626-33, 637, 641-43, 644-50; Louis-André Vigneras, ''Diego Méndez, Secretary of Christopher Columbus and Alguacil Mayor of Santo Domingo: A Biographical Sketch,'' *Hispanic American Historical Review* 58 (1978): 676-96.

MENDOZA, DON PEDRO GONZALES DE (1428-1495)

Archbishop of Toledo and Grand Cardinal of Spain. Fourth son of Inigo López de Mendoza, Marquess of Santillana and Duke of Infantado. Mendoza was born in Guadalajara, New Castile, of a family distinguished for centuries for its loyalty and service to the crown of **Castile.** He was sent into the Church because he was a younger son and, in 1454, he was made bishop of Calahorra, a post that also made him the civil and military leader of the town and its dependent district. He had two sons, Rodrigo and Diego, by Doña Mónica de Lemus and another by a woman of a **Valladolid** family. In 1468 he became bishop of Siguenza, and in 1473 was made Archbishop of **Seville,** Cardinal, and Chancellor of Castile. He took the side of Princess **Isabel** during the last years of Henry IV. He fought for her at the battle of Toro in March 1476, was instrumental in placing her on the throne, and vigorously supported her efforts to suppress the turbulent nobles of Castile. In 1482 he became Archbishop of Toledo. He contributed extensively to the maintenance of the army of Castile and **Aragón** during the conquest of **Granada** and occupied the city in the name of the Spanish monarchs. He acted as intermediary between the papacy and the Spanish sovereigns in various disputes. Though worldly, he did not neglect his duties as bishop. He gave extensively to charity and endowed the College of Santa Cruz at Valladolid.

Ref. *AOS*1 I, 115, II, 14-15, 49; *AOS*2, 87, 100, 360-61.

Mina, San Jorge da

A Portuguese stone castle on the Gold Coast of Africa at about the point where the coast turns west. The castle was built in the winter of 1481/82 by an expedition commissioned by King **John II** and commanded by **Diogo d'Azambuja.** Its purpose was to protect Portuguese trading, mining, and **slaving** interest on the west African coast from rival European powers and from the native peoples. CC claims, in marginal notes nos. 16, 234, and 490 in his copy of *Imago Mundi*, to have visited Mina.

Ref. *AOS*1 I, 53-55, 59; *AOS*2, 41-42, 110; Alberto Salvagnini, "Colombo e i corsari Colombo suoi conteporanei," *Raccolta di documenti e studi pubblicati dalla R. Commissione colombiana pel quarto centenario della scoperta dell'America,* vol. 2 (Rome: Ministro della Pubblica Istruzione, 1892-96), 294, 375, 390, 407.

Moguer

One of the towns, along with **Huelva** and **Palos de la Frontera,** in the region of southwestern **Spain** designated as the Condado de **Niebla.** The town of Moguer is near the River **Tinto** about three miles northeast of **Palos.**

Moluccas

The **Spice Islands** that CC attempted to reach by sailing west. The Portuguese and the Spanish under **Magellan** did reach them, the former by sailing east around Africa and the latter by sailing west around South **America.** *See* **East Indies.**

Molyart, Miguel (n.d.)

The husband of CC's sister-in-law Violante (or Briolante) **Moniz,** who lived with his wife in **Huelva** not far from **Palos.** It is possible, but not certain, that CC left his son **Diego** in the Molyarts' care while the child was being schooled by the Franciscans at **La Rábida** in the years prior to the **First Voyage.**

Ref. *AOS*1 I, 58, 103.

Moniz, Violante (Briolante)
See **Molyart, Miguel.**

Moniz Family

The prominent Portuguese noble family into which CC married. His mother-in-law, Isabel Moniz, was descended from Egas Moniz, governor under the first Portuguese king, Afonso Enriquez. The family was on good terms with the crown right down to CC's time, and it seems reasonable that this connection was the path by which CC obtained an audience with King **John II** in about 1484 to offer his **Enterprise of the Indies** to **Portugal.** However, it also seems likely that by the time CC married **Felipa Perestrello e Moniz** in about 1479, Felipa's widowed mother had fallen on straitened circumstances, since both Felipa and her sister Violante (or Briolante) married commoners.

Ref. *AOS*1 I, 50-52, 58; *AOS*2, 37-39; A.M. Freitas and Regina Maney, *The Wife of Columbus* (New York: Stettiner, 1893); Henry Vignaud, *Études critiques sur la vie de Colomb avant ses découvertes* (Paris: Welter, 1905), 424-504.

MONSERRAT

An island in the **Lesser Antilles,** northwest of **Guadeloupe,** which CC discovered on 11 November 1493 on the **Third Voyage** and named Santa María de Monserrate. The island, never settled by the Spanish, was occupied by the British in the 1800s.

Ref. *AOS*1 II, 73; *AOS*2, 410.

MONTEGO BAY

A spacious bay on the northwest coast of **Jamaica,** discovered by CC on 9 May 1494, during the **Second Voyage.** He named it El Golfo de Buen Tiempo, the Gulf of Good Weather.

Ref. *AOS*1 II, 125, 154; *AOS*2, 453, 474.

MOORS

The general term given to the Moslem, Arabic-speaking people of Arab and Berber descent who crossed from Morocco, invaded and settled in the **Iberian Peninsula** in the eighth century A.D. The Christian native peoples of the peninsula, after seven centuries of intermittent effort, and headed by **Ferdinand** and **Isabel,** drove out the Moorish inhabitants at **Granada** on 2 January 1492, after which the **Catholic Monarchs** turned their attention to CC's **Enterprise of the Indies.** Today the Spanish refer to the Moslem inhabitants of the Philippine Islands as *Moros* (Spanish for Moors), a throwback to the time when the Spanish equated any Moslem enemies with the former Moorish occupants of the Iberian Peninsula.

Ref. Lee Anne Durham Seminario, *The History of the Blacks, the Jews and the Moors in Spain,* (Madrid: Playor S.A., 1975), 73-105.

MORALES, ALONSO DE (n.d.)

The treasurer of **Castile** at the time of CC's **Fourth Voyage.** He apparently forced CC to accept **Francisco** and Diego **de Porras,** brothers of his mistress (the latter an auditor), as crew members of the **Bermuda**, known formally as **Santiago de Palos.** Francisco served as captain. These brothers later rebelled against CC during the mutiny while the crews were stranded on **Jamaica.** Morales also seems to have been instrumental in causing King **Ferdinand**'s irritation with CC after the death of Queen **Isabel,** which may have resulted in some loss to CC's estate during his final years.

Ref. *AOS*1 II, 320, 398, 413, 417; *AOS*2, 585, 662, 666.

MOUSTIQUE BAY

CC raised a cross on 12 December 1492 on the western cape of this inlet in northwestern **Hispaniola,** claiming the island for the Spanish monarchs.

Ref. *AOS*1 I, 370-72; *AOS*2, 283-85.

MOXICA, ADRIAN DEO (n.d.)

A supporter of **Francisco de Roldán** and his rebellion against CC in 1498/99, he began a rebellion of his own in the summer of 1499 after Roldán had elicited highly favorable terms for himself from CC and settled with him. CC, overly lenient with Roldán, put down the Moxica rebellion vigorously and hanged seven rebels in sight of the harbor. They were seen there by the arriving **Francisco de Bobadilla,** justice of **Spain,** whom the Spanish monarchs had sent at CC's request. Bobadilla, appalled by this sight and by information picked up from the inhabitants, jailed CC and **Bartholomew Columbus** and sent them home in chains to face the monarchs.

Ref. *AOS*1 II, 302.

MOYA, MARQUESA DE (n.d.)

Beatriz de Bobadilla, a close friend of Queen **Isabel** and cousin of the notorious **Beatriz de Bobadilla y Pereza,** King **Ferdinand**'s mistress. The Marquesa de Moya is thought by some to have helped persuade Queen Isabel to reconsider CC's proposal after the fall of **Granada.**

Ref. *AOS*1 I, 144, 211-16; R.B. Merriman, *The Rise of the Spanish Empire in the Old World and the New,* vol. 2 (New York: Macmillan, 1936), chap. 16 *passim;* Henry Vignaud, *Études critiques sur la vie de Colomb avant ses découvertes,* vol. 2 (Paris: Welter, 1905), 76-89.

MÜNTZER, HIERONYMUS (n.d.)

The German astronomer who wrote to King **John II** of **Portugal** on 14 July 1493, four months after CC's successful return from the **West Indies,** urging him to mount a voyage of discovery westward to China which he could, Müntzer claimed, reach in only a few days.

Ref. *AOS*1 I, 100, 141; *AOS*2, 77-78, 107.

N

NAO

See CARRACK.

NAVIDAD

A makeshift fort on the northwest coast of **Hispaniola,** begun about 25 December 1492, constructed from the timbers of the wrecked *Santa María.* For lack of room on the return voyage, CC left approximately forty crew members of the **First Voyage** at Navidad. This, the first European colony in the **West Indies,** was destroyed by **Indians** and its entire garrison massacred shortly before CC returned to the site on the **Second Voyage. Bartolomé de Las Casas** attributed the anger of the Indians to a group of the Spanish colonists who roamed the island raping and looting. *See* CAONABÓ, RODRIGO DE ESCOBEDO, and PEDRO DE GUTIÉRREZ.

Ref. *AOS*1 I, 190-92, 393-94, II, 91-95; *AOS*2, 305-407, 423-28.

NAVIGATION

Although CC had a **quadrant** for determining **latitude** by reading the elevation of the sun or of a star, he did not use the instrument successfully for navigation. He sailed by dead reckoning, or, in other words, by keeping track of the ship's direction by means of a compass, and of the estimated speed of the ship, and plotting these daily on a chart. CC's daily record of the **First Voyage** is recorded in **Bartolomé de Las Casas**'s abstract of the *Journal.* In spite of the obvious limitations of these procedures in a turbulent sea, CC was a highly successful navigator, justly reputed as the greatest of deadreckoners, one who apparently could respond very accurately to whatever clues were available.

Some scholars attribute CC's success in crossing the Atlantic on a chosen parallel to "**latitude sailing**"—aiming at a point on the horizon determined by the positions of selected stars as they rise each night. The *Journal* says nothing of this, and he did navigate with remarkable precision even when the sea was stormy and the stars not visible. On the return leg of the First Voyage, stormy most of the way, he made **landfall** at the mouth of the **Tagus River** less than 100 miles north of his target, a tiny error after a voyage of 800 miles from the **Azores.**

Ref. *AOS1* I, 240-63; Georges A. Charlier, *Étude complète de la navigation et de l'itineraire de Cristóbal Colón lors de son voyage de découverte de l'Amérique* (Liège: Charlier, 1988); F.A. McNutt, trans., *De Orbe Novo, the Eight Decades of Peter Martyr d'Anghiera* (New York and London: G.P. Putnam, 1912).

NEGRO, PAOLO DI (n.d.)

A Genoese native, scion of the di Negro family of maritime merchants, who represented the family concern in **Lisbon** during and after CC's years in **Portugal.** He hired CC as a seagoing agent and, in 1478, sent him to **Funchal, Madeira** to purchase sugar for another Genoese concern, the firm of **Centurione.** Because of some defect in the arrangements, CC ultimately had to testify in court in **Genoa** about the resulting misunderstanding between the Centurione and di Negro firms. Whatever CC's feelings about this incident, it did not destroy the relationship completely, since he left money to Paolo di Negro in his will. *See ASSERETO DOCUMENT.*

Ref. *AOS1* I, 30-31; Ugo Assereto, "La data della nascità di Colombo accertata da un documento nuovo," *Giornale Storico e Letterario Liguriano* (Genoa) 5 (1904): 5-16, a copy of the original document; *JOD,* 8-9, an English translation of the Assereto document.

NEWFOUNDLAND

The Canadian island northeast of Maine that **John Cabot** discovered for **Henry VII** of **England** in 1497. This was the first non-Spanish European discovery of lands in the western Atlantic to result from CC's discovery of the **Bahamas** and the **West Indies.** It is quite possible, however, that the Portuguese had been fishing the Grand Banks off Newfoundland for many years; the Portuguese were notoriously secretive about their fifteenth-century Atlantic voyages.

NEW WORLD

The term for the area of CC's discoveries, coined by **Peter Martyr,** whose Latin verse account of the Spanish voyages, including CC's, was entitled *De Orbe Novo,* "Of the New World," in the 1516 edition. CC himself uses the term "another world" to describe the mouth of the **Orinoco** in his journal of the **Third Voyage.**

Ref. *AOS1* II, 40, 268-69; *AOS2,* 383-84, 547-48; John Fiske, *The Discovery of America with Some Account of Ancient America and the Spanish Conquests,* 2 vols. (Boston and New York: Houghton Mifflin, 1892), gives special emphasis to the evolution of the concept of the "New World"; Juan Valera, "Concepción progresivo del nuevo mundo," *El Centenario* (Madrid) 3 (1893): 145-55.

NIEBLA, CONDADO DE

A flat region of southwestern **Spain,** near the Portuguese border, where the town of **Palos de la Frontera** is located, as well as the towns of **Huelva** and **Moguer.** The area is drained by the **Tinto** and **Odiel** rivers, which join near Palos to form the **Saltes.** CC embarked on the **First Voyage** from Palos on the Tinto and followed the Saltes into the Atlantic Ocean.

Ref. *AOS*1 I, 107-9; *AOS*2, 79-82, 142, 586.

NIÑA

One of the three vessels constituting CC's fleet on the **First Voyage.** The *Niña* was owned by Juan Niño (see **Niño Family**) of **Moguer,** who sailed as master on the **ship.** It was commanded by **Vicente Yañez Pinzón** (brother of **Martín Alonso Pinzón**) until CC took command after the wreck of the *Santa María* off the northwest coast of **Hispaniola** on 24 December 1492. CC returned to **Palos** in the *Niña* on 15 March 1493, completing the First Voyage. There was a ship called *Niña* (official name *Santa Clara*) on the **Second Voyage** which CC used to explore **Jamaica** and the southern coast of **Cuba** in the spring of 1494, and in which he returned to **Spain** (along with the *India*) from 10 March to 11 June 1496. Morison thinks the *Niña*s of the First and Second Voyages are the same ship. While this remains controversial, it may be significant that Francisco Niño, brother

of the 1492 owner Juan Niño, was pilot of the *Niña* on the Second Voyage.

A ship *Niña,* official name *Santa Clara,* probably the same as the *Niña* of the Second Voyage, was recruited for the **Third Voyage;** this one was sent ahead to Hispaniola with supplies before the departure of the main fleet. This *Niña* was carrying a "countermizzen" sail in its supply locker, presumably an indication that it had four masts instead of the usual three.

Ref. *AOS*2, 114-17, 139-48, 163-64, 204, 272, 298-302, 316-53, 395-96, 445-77, 491, 496-501, 511-12; José María Martínez-Hidalgo, "Las naves de los cuatro viajes de Colón al nuevo mundo," *Temi Colombiani* (Genoa: ECIG, 1986), 201-29; Eugene Lyon, "Fifteenth-Century Manuscript Yields First Look at *Niña,*" *National Geographic* 170 (November 1986): 601-05.

NIÑO FAMILY

A prominent seafaring family of the town of **Moguer,** just north of **Palos** on the **Tinto** River. Juan Niño owned the *Niña* and sailed as master of the **ship** on the **First Voyage.** He was a favorite of CC, who took Niño to the reception given by the **Catholic Monarchs** in **Barcelona** in the spring of 1493. Peralonso Niño went as pilot on the *Santa María* on the same voyage and Francisco Niño was a gromet. Francisco sailed as pilot on the *Niña* of the **Second Voyage** and also went on the **Fourth Voyage.** Other members of the family, including Cristóbal Pérez Niño and another Francisco Niño, also sailed on CC's **Third** and Fourth Voyages.

Ref. *AOS1* I, 181-82, II, 56; *AOS2*, 139, 205, 211, 223, 321-22, 396, 501, 562, 568-69.

NORONHA, MARTIN DE (n.d.)

A highly placed Portuguese noble who conducted CC and his entourage to the retreat of King **John II** of **Portugal.** CC had landed at **Restelo,** on the **Tagus River** below **Lisbon,** where the *Niña* anchored after arriving from the **West Indies** on 4 March 1493. The retreat of King John was at Virtudes, northeast of Lisbon.

Ref. *AOS1* I, 436-43; *JOD,* 176-78.

O

O'BRASIL

One of the many mythical islands that medieval legends placed in the Atlantic. O'Brasil was supposed to be west of **Ireland.**

Ref. *AOS*1 I, 80-81; *AOS*2, 58.

ODIEL RIVER

The river that joins the **Tinto** just south of **Palos de la Frontera** to form the **Saltes.** The town of **Huelva** near Palos is on the Odiel, where CC's sister-in-law Violante (or Briolante) Perestrello **Molyart,** and her husband, Miguel, resided when CC arrived in **Spain** around 1485.

Ref. *AOS*1 I, 107, 209.

OJEDA

See **HOJEDA, ALONSO DE.**

ORIENTE PROVINCE

The easternmost province of **Cuba,** credited as the site of CC's discovery of the island on 28 October 1492, on the northeast shore that he called **San Salvador.** CC explored the coast and some of the inland country from 28 October to 5 December 1492. During the **Second Voyage,** from 29 April to 3 May 1494, CC explored the southern coast of Oriente Province from Cape Alpha and Omega to Cape **Cruz,** discovering both **Guantanamo Bay** and the site of the future city of Santiago.

Ref. *AOS*2, 254-79, 447-51; Luis Morales Pedroso, *Lugar donde Colón desembarcó por primera vez en Cuba* (Havana: Sociedad Geografía de Cuba, 1923).

ORINOCO RIVER

A large river flowing through **Venezuela** and northeastern South **America.** CC discovered one of the major mouths of the river at the **Gulf of Paría** southwest of **Trinidad** on the **Third Voyage** in August 1498. CC had sensed that the enormous flood of fresh water must have indicated a continent but historians disagree about whether he therefore ceased to think that he was in the Orient.

Ref. *AOS*1 II, 254-93; *AOS*2, 533-37; Kirkpatrick Sale, *The Conquest of Paradise* (New York: Knopf, 1990), chap. 7 *passim.*

OVANDO, NICOLÁS DE (ca. 1460-1518)

An administrator whom the Spanish sovereigns appointed to succeed CC as governor of **Hispaniola** on 3 September 1501, an act that suspended some of CC's rights and privileges as granted by the **Capitulations of 1492.** Ovando achieved peace among the contending factions in Hispaniola, but he steadfastly refused to aid CC or have any dealings with him whatsoever. When CC arrived at **Santo Domingo** harbor on the **Fourth Voyage,** Ovando refused CC permission for his fleet to take shelter in the harbor from an approaching **storm.** Ovando also ignored CC's message that the treasure fleet of thirty vessels in the harbor should not be dispatched because of the storm. As a result, nineteen of the **ships** were lost with all hands. Only one ship, the *Aguja,* reached **Spain;** the others were all sunk or disabled. Later, during the Fourth Voyage, when CC was stranded on **Jamaica,** Ovando declined to rescue him and CC's aide **Diego Méndez** had to hire a ship to Santo Domingo and effect the rescue himself.

Ref. *AOS*1 II, 303-413; *AOS*2, 580-90, 649-62, 666; Clarence H. Haring, "The Genesis of Royal Government in the Spanish Indies," *Hispanic American Historical Review* 7 (1927): 141-91.

OVIEDO Y VALDÉS, GONZALO FERNÁNDEZ (1478-1557)

Oviedo wrote one of four contemporary, fairly comprehensive accounts of CC and his voyages. He was a friend of the Spanish prince, the **Infante Don Juan;** in the war of Naples he fought under Gonsalve de Córdova. He went to Darién in 1513 with Pedrarios Davila as comptroller of **gold** diggings and made the rest of his career in the **New World.** Ovieda was the official chronicler of the **Indies** and author of the *Historia General y Natural de las Indias,* a main source for information on the life of CC. The book contains excellent commentary on **navigation** and on the natural features of the New World, illustrated by the author's own sketches. *See* **FERDINAND COLUMBUS, BARTOLOMÉ DE LAS CASAS,** and **PETER MARTYR.**

Ref. *AOS*1 I, 61-62, 71-75, 83-84, II, 181, 200-203, 304; *AOS*2, 43-44, 51-52, 61-62, 149, 220, 572; Antonello Gerbi, *La natura delle Indie nove. Da Cristoforo Colombo a Gonzalo Fernández de Oviedo* (Milan and Naples: Ricciardi, 1975); Jeremy Moylet, *Nature in the New World: From Christopher Columbus to Oviedo* (Pittsburgh: University of Pittsburgh Press, 1986), an English translation; Gonzalo Fernández Oviedo y Valdés, *Historia General y Natural de las Indias,* 4 vols. (Madrid: 1851-1855).

OZAMA RIVER

The river in southeastern **Hispaniola** at the mouth of which is built the capital city **Santo Domingo.**

P

PALMA ISLAND
See CANARY ISLANDS.

PALMAS, LAS
See LAS PALMAS.

PALOS DE LA FRONTERA

The town in southwestern **Spain** on the **Tinto** River where CC may have made his first entry into Spain around 1485. The town is just north of the Franciscan friary of **La Rábida.** Historians who think he reached Palos in 1485 say that CC was befriended by the friars at La Rábida. He may have left his son **Diego** there while soliciting aid for his **Enterprise of the Indies** from the Spanish sovereigns with the assistance of the Franciscan **Antonio de Marchena.** In 1491, when CC had despaired of aid from the crown of Spain, he returned to Palos to take Diego to France with him. He was persuaded not to leave Spain by **Fray Juan Pérez,** then at La Rábida, who visited his former penitent, Queen **Isabel,** and persuaded her to resume negotiations with CC.

When CC had been commissioned to make the **First Voyage,** the prominent mariner of Palos, **Martín Alonso Pinzón,** took a deep interest in the project. He was instrumental in assembling an excellent crew and was no doubt responsible for selecting the remarkably seaworthy *Pinta* and *Niña* as the two **caravels** that the town was required by the sovereigns to provide for the voyage. Pinzón himself commanded the *Pinta* and his brother, **Vicente Yañez Pinzón,** commanded the *Niña.* CC's fleet sailed from Palos on the Great Voyage of Discovery on 3 August 1492; the *Niña,* with CC, and the *Pinta* returned to Palos after the successful voyage on 14 March 1493.

Ref. *AOS*2, 109-14, 149-58, 352-53.

PANAMA

The discovery of the site of this Central American republic occurred in October 1502, on CC's **Fourth Voyage,** when he was sailing along the Central American coast, searching for a strait to the Indian Ocean. CC explored the area until 1503, attempted a settlement at the mouth of the **Belén** River, and finally abandoned the effort to find a strait.

Ref. *AOS*1 II, 342-81, 360-61 (map 2); *AOS*2, 605-36.

PANÉ, RAMÓN (n.d.)

A Jeronymite priest who accompanied CC on the **Second Voyage.** He was responsible for the first conversion and baptism of an **Indian** on 21 September 1496, three years after **Fray Bernal Buil** had been charged with the task of converting the Indians of **Hispaniola** and seeing to their spiritual welfare. Fray Pané also founded American anthropology with his carefully observed account of the native Americans, published as an insert in **Ferdinand Columbus**'s life of CC, the *Historie.*

> Ref. *AOS1* II, 342-81 *passim; AOS2*, 397, 484; Demetrio Ramos Pérez, "Sobre la 'relacion' de Pané dedicada a los taínos y su utilización por Martír de Anglería en 1497," *Archivio Hispalense* (Seville) 68, nos. 207 and 208 (1985): 419-29. Pané's report on the Indians.

PAPAL BULLS

Popes Sixtus IV and **Alexander VI** both issued bulls regulating the relationships between **Spain** and **Portugal** in Atlantic explorations. In 1481 Sixtus IV issued the bull *Aeterni Regis,* which confirmed the **Treaty of Alcáçovas** of 1479 between Spain and Portugal.

After CC's return from the **First Voyage** in 1493, the Spanish Borgia pope, Alexander VI, granted certain privileges to Spain vis-à-vis Portugal. These privileges are defined in five papal bulls of 1493, most notably *Inter Caetera II* of 4 May (*see* **Carvajal, Bernardino de**), which established the famous **demarcation line** between Spanish and Portuguese areas of conquest. Alexander's other pertinent bulls were *Eximiae Devotionis* of 3 May 1493, *Inter Caetera I* of 3 May, *Pius Fidelium* of 25 June, and *Dudum Siquidem* of 26 September. The cumulative response to these bulls led to the Treaty of Tordesillas in 1494, which fixed the Line of Demarcation in the Atlantic between the explored territories of the Spanish and the Portuguese.

> Ref. *AOS1* I, 439, II, 22-29; *AOS2*, 344, 368-74; Edward Gaylord Bourne, "The History and Determination of the Line of Demarcation Established by Pope Alexander VI, between the Spanish and Portuguese Fields of Discovery and Colonization," *Yale Review* 1 (1892): 33-55; H. Van der Linden, "Alexander VI and the Demarcation of the Maritime and Colonial Domains of Spain and Portugal, 1493-1494," *American Historical Review* 22 (1916-17): 1-20.

PARÍA, GULF OF

The body of water between **Trinidad** and the Paría Peninsula into which a major northern distributary of the **Orinoco River** empties. CC discovered the Gulf of Paría on 2 August 1498 on the **Third Voyage,** entering through the **Boca de la Sierpe** just south of Trinidad. CC called the Gulf the "Golfo de la Ballena"—The Gulf of the Whale—for a reason that is not known, but probably because he sighted a whale at the time.

Ref. *AOS1* II, 253-56; *AOS2*, 534-53.

PEARL COAST

The name given to the stretch of Venezuelan Caribbean coast west of the mouth of the **Orinoco River** where, in 1500, Peralonso **Niño** collected a cargo of pearls, opening up a wealthy pearl fishery that **Spain** exploited throughout the sixteenth century. CC came within a few miles of the Pearl Coast during his **Third Voyage,** on 15 August 1498, as he left for **Hispaniola** after discovering **Trinidad** and the mouth of the Orinoco.

A narrative document gives an account of five **caravels,** sent south from Hispaniola by CC, discovering **Venezuela** and the pearl fishery and making a circuit of the Caribbean in 1494. The document was allegedly sent to Venice by **Angelo Trevisan** in 1502. It has been used to show that CC deliberately concealed the discovery from the crown, intending perhaps to exploit it for his own benefit at a later time.

Ref. *AOS1* II, 278-81; *AOS2*, 546-53; Charles E. Nowell, "Reservations Regarding the Historicity of the 1494 Discovery of South America," *Hispanic American*

Historical Review 22 (1942): 205-10; W.J. Wilson, "The Spanish Discovery of the South American Mainland," *Geographical Review* 31 (1941): 283-99.

PERAZA, BEATRIZ DE BOBADILLA Y
See BOBADILLA Y PERAZA, BEATRIZ DE (OF GOMERA).

PERESTRELLO E MONIZ, FELIPA (ca. 1454-ca. 1485)

The daughter of Bartholomew **Perestrello** and his third wife, Isabel **Moniz.** Not much is known about CC's wife. They met while attending mass at the Convento dos Santos in **Lisbon** and were probably married sometime before late 1479. After a short stay in Lisbon, they left for **Porto Santo,** where their only child, **Diego Columbus,** was born about 1480. Information about her death is sketchy, but she probably died before CC left **Portugal** in 1485.

Ref. *AOS2*, 37-40, 85, 342, 588.

PERESTRELLO FAMILY

A family originally from the Italian city of Piacenza who settled in **Portugal** and enjoyed the favor of the throne during much of the fifteenth century. CC married a member of the family, **Felipa Perestrello e Moniz.** *See* PORTO SANTO.

Ref. *AOS1* I, 49-51, 58; *AOS2*, 29, 37-39; A.M. Freitas and Regina Maney, *The Wife of Columbus* (New York: Stettiner, 1893); Salvador de Madariaga, *Christopher*

Columbus (New York: Oxford University Press, 1939), 84-86, 138; Henry Vignaud, *Études critiques sur la vie de Colomb avant ses découvertes* (Paris: Welter, 1905), 424.

PÉREZ, FRAY JUAN (d. ca. 1512)

A Franciscan priest who, in 1491, journeyed from the friary of **La Rábida** to the siege fortress of the **Catholic Monarchs** at **Santa Fé** and successfully persuaded Queen **Isabel** to reconsider CC's **Enterprise of the Indies.** Fray Pérez is supposed to have been the prior of La Rábida at the time CC first came to **Spain** in 1485, and is thought to have put CC in touch with **Fray Antonio de Marchena,** a Franciscan astronomer who helped CC establish contact with the crown; the evidence for the presence of Pérez at La Rábida in 1485 is not strong, however.

Ref. *AOS*1 I, 108-46; *AOS*2, 80-81, 99-104. *AOS* is somewhat dated in its references to the presence of Fr. Pérez at La Rábida in 1485. Juan Manzano Manzano, *Cristóbal Colón: siete años decisivos de su vida, 1485-1492* (Madrid: Ediciones Cultura Hispánica, 1964); Antonio Rumeu de Armas, *La Rábida y el descubrimiento de América: Colón, Marchena, y fray Juan Pérez* (Madrid: Cultura Hispánica, 1968).

PICCOLOMINI, ENEA SILVIO
See SYLVIUS, AENEAS.

PINA, RUY DE (d. 1519)

A court chronicler for King **John II** of **Portugal** at the time of CC's audience with King John, in March 1493, at the monastery of **Santa Maria das Virtudes.** CC had taken refuge from an Atlantic **storm** in the **Lisbon** harbor after his return crossing during the **First Voyage.** Because of Pina's report, perhaps made as an eyewitness, we have an account of the meeting in considerable detail.

Ref. *AOS*1 I, 439-44; *JOD,* 177, a translation of Ruy de Pina's report.

PINELLI, FRANCESCO (n.d.)

A merchant and banker of Genoese birth who was already well established in **Spain** when CC arrived with references which were perhaps from other Ligurians in **Portugal.** Pinelli was, with **Luis de Santangel,** the co-treasurer of the **Santa Hermandad** and a trusted counselor of King **Ferdinand.** He was related through marriage to the **Centurione** family, Genoese merchant-bankers with branches throughout Spain.

Pinelli was in large part responsible for the funding of CC's voyages, both personally and through friends and relatives, and was one of the merchants who actively traded with the **West Indies.**

Ref. A. Boscolo, "II Genovese

Francesco Pinelli,'' *Presencia Italiana en Andalucia, Siglos XIV-XVII,* Actas del I Coloquio Hispano-Italiano, 1983 (Seville: Escuela de Estudios Hispanoaméricanos, 1985), 249-66.

PINTA

One of the three **ships** in CC's fleet of discovery on the **First Voyage** from 1492 to 1493. The *Pinta,* like the *Niña,* was furnished to the expedition by the town of **Palos** under a royal penalty, and both appear to have been constructed locally; the *Pinta* was, in fact, owned by a local sailor named **Quintero.** The square-rigged *Pinta,* at fifty-five tons and seventy feet in length, was the fastest of the three ships, carried a crew of twenty-six, and was commanded by **Martín Alonso Pinzón,** an influential sea captain of Palos and CC's chief resource in assembling fleet and crew. Pinzón became his rival and enemy in the course of the voyage however. The *Pinta*'s rudder jumped its gudgeons on the first leg of the voyage and had to be repaired at **Las Palmas** on **Grand Canary Island.** Like the *Niña,* the *Pinta* returned successfully from the **West Indies,** making **landfall** at the northern Spanish harbor of **Bayona** and reaching Palos within hours of the *Niña,* both on 15 March 1493. Nothing certain is known of the *Pinta*'s subsequent history.

Ref. *AOS*1 I, 154-73; *AOS*2, 117-18, 138-49; C. Etayo Elizondo, *La Santa María, la Niña, y la Pinta* (Pamplona: Isuna, 1962); Alicia Bache Gould, *Nueva lista documentada de los tripulantes de Colón en 1492,* ed. José de la Peña y Camara (Madrid: Real Academia de la Historia, 1984); José María Martínez-Hidalgo, *Columbus' Ships,* ed. Howard I. Chapelle (Barre, MA: Barre Publishers, 1966); José María Martínez-Hidalgo, ''Las naves de Colón y la polémica que no cesa,'' *Revista General de Marina* (Madrid) 211 (1986): 477-95.

PINZÓN, MARTÍN ALONSO (1441-1493)

The head of a seafaring family in **Palos,** Pinzón was instrumental in helping CC assemble the fleet and the crew for the **First Voyage.** Martín Alonso, an experienced and skillful navigator, commanded the **caravel** *Pinta* and, until the **landfall** at **Guanahani,** was a useful counselor, aiding CC in quieting a potential mutiny on board the *Santa María.* CC, however, recorded a lack of trust in him before the fleet reached the **Canary Islands** and, after the landfall, the two men fell out over Pinzón's decision to leave the fleet and explore the north coast of **Hispaniola** on his own.

After the wreck of the *Santa María* on 24 December 1492, Pinzón, in the *Pinta,* rejoined the *Niña* and the two **ships** set out for **Spain** together.

Pinzón's ship was separated from the *Niña* in a **storm** and returned to Spain alone, making landfall at the northern Spanish port of **Bayona.** Perhaps feeling that CC had not survived the voyage, he notified the **Catholic Monarchs,** then in **Barcelona,** of his return and may have been refused permission to report to them personally. He then sailed on to Palos, arriving on 15 March 1493, only hours after CC arrived in the *Niña* on the same date. Pinzón was extremely ill when he arrived and died a few days later in the care of the Franciscans in the friary of **La Rábida.**

Some have conjectured that Pinzón was so disappointed to find that CC had returned that he died of a broken heart. Others feel that he contracted **syphilis** in Hispaniola and was mortally ill of the disease when he returned to Spain, noting a reference by **Ruy de Isla** in his *Tractado contra el mal serpentino* (*Treatise against syphilis,* Seville, 1539) to a "pilot called Pinçón," who contracted the malady on CC's First Voyage.

Ref. *AOS*1 II, 3-5; *AOS*2, 99, 135-38, 160, 207, 212-21, 226, 259, 268-70, 306-9, 326, 350-52; Ana María Manzano Fernández-Heredia and Juan Manzano Manzano, *Los Pinzones y el descubrimiento de América,* vol. 1 (Madrid: Ediciones Cultural Hispánica, 1988); Angel Ortega, *La Rábida: historia documental críti-* ca, vol. 3 (Seville: Editorial de San Antonio, 1925-26); F. Morales Padrón, "Las Relaciones entre Colón y Martín Alonso Pinzón," *Revista de Indias* (Madrid) 3 (1961): 95-106.

PINZÓN, VICENTE YAÑEZ (1460-1524)
A younger brother of **Martín Alonso Pinzón.** Vicente commanded the *Niña* on the **First Voyage** until the flagship *Santa María* was wrecked off **Haiti** on Christmas Eve 1492; after that CC sailed aboard the *Niña* and commanded it. Beginning in 1499, after the **Catholic Monarchs** ceased to honor CC's exclusive right to control the exploration of the **Indies,** Vicente became a leader in the exploration of South **America,** discovering the mouth of the Amazon. Later he was, for a time, governor of part of the mainland of South America along the Caribbean.

Ref. *AOS*2, 136, 139, 217-20, 270, 301, 309, 320-21, 569; Ana María Manzano Fernández-Heredia and Juan Manzano Manzano, *Los Pinzones y el descubrimiento de América,* 3 vols. (Madrid: Ediciones Cultural Hispánica, 1988); Angel Ortega, *La Rábida: historia documental crítica,* vol. 3 (Seville: Editorial de San Santonio, 1925-26).

PINZÓN FAMILY
The name of the seafaring family in **Palos** to which belonged four members of CC's **First Voyage: Martín**

Alonso, Vicente Yañez, and Francisco Martín Pinzón, all brothers, and a cousin, Diego Martín Pinzón.

Ref. *AOS1* I, 178-81; *AOS2*, 135-39; Ana María Manzano Fernández-Heredia and Juan Manzano Manzano, *Los Pinzones y el descubrimiento de América,* 3 vols. (Madrid: Ediciones Cultural Hispánica, 1988); Angel Ortega, *La Rábida: historia documental crítica,* vol. 3 (Seville: Editorial de San Antonio, 1925-26).

Piri Re'is map
An early sixteenth-century Turkish world map made by Piri Re'is (ca. 1470-1554), an Ottoman cartographer. A legend on the map attributes the representation of the **West Indies** to a map made by "the Genoese infidel Colombo" which was seized on a captured ship. This is one of many pieces of contemporary evidence that CC was Genoese. The rendering of the **Lesser Antilles** from **Monserrat** to **Dominica** is very accurate on this map. This is the part of the **Indies** that CC sailed through when he returned on his **Second Voyage.** The rest of the representation of the Indies on this map is of no account.

Ref. *AOS1* I, 171-72; *AOS2*, 408-9; A. Afetinan, *Life and Works of Piri Re'is: The Oldest Map of America,* trans. Leman Yolaç and Engin Uzmen, 2nd. ed. (Ankara: Atatürk Supreme Council for Cul-

ture, Language and History, Publications of Turkish Historical Society), 9, 26-39, 39-42; P.E. Kahle, "A Lost Map of Columbus," *Geographical Review* 23 (1933): 621-38.

Pius II, Pope
See Sylvius, Aeneas.

Pius Fidelium
See papal bulls.

Pleitos de Colón, Los
See Los Pleitos de Colón

Polo, Marco (ca. 1254-1324)
The Venetian traveler to China whose book describing his travels, *Il Milione,* or *The Book of Ser Marco Polo,* was transcribed at Polo's dictation by a certain Rusticiano or Rusticello of Pisa. At the time, both were prisoners of the Genoese, taken during the Battle of Curzola Bay in the Adriatic in 1298. The **Enterprise of the Indies** has long been reputed to have been inspired, in part, by CC's reading of Marco Polo; his copy of *Il Milione,* still available for study in **Seville** (but see cautionary word under **Biblioteca Colombina**), is elaborately annotated in CC's hand. At the time of the **First Voyage,** CC was familiar with names and phrases used by Marco Polo, which he sometimes used in his *Journal of the First Voyage.* Nonetheless, the paucity of these phrases in the *Journal* and the failure to refer more specifically to Polo has led to questions about whether CC actual-

ly read the book before the First Voyage.

In 1956, when a 1497 letter appeared from the Englishman **John Day** to "The Admiral of Spain" (very possibly meaning CC) mentioning a copy of *Marco Polo* that Day was sending, certain modern scholars began to consider the possibility that this book was the one annotated by CC. The most vocal of these scholars, Juan Gil of Seville, holds that CC's annotations were not made as a part of his reading prior to his voyage of discovery, but in order to prepare to defend himself against detractors who attacked him on various grounds after he became successful.

Ref. *Encyclopedia Britannica*, 11th ed., s.v. "Marco Polo"; Juan Gil, ed. and trans, *El libro de Marco Polo anotado por Cristóbal Colón. El libro de Marco Polo: version de Rodrigo de Santiella* (Madrid: Alianza, 1987), contains (1) the first Latin edition of 1485, the one owned and annotated by CC: both the Latin text and CC's notes are translated into Spanish; (2) the first Castilian translation of *Marco Polo* (Seville, 1519), made by Rodrigo Fernández de Santaella from the 1503 Venetian edition of the Latin text. Gil's introductory essay (i-lxix) places all this within the context of Seville at the turn of the sixteenth century. Gil concludes (viii) that CC did not own or anno-

tate Marco Polo's book until 1497; L.A. Vigneras, "The Cape Breton Landfall: 1494 or 1497? Note on a Letter from John Day," *Canadian Historical Review* 38 (1957): 219-29, contains an English translation of the Day letter and a discussion of CC vis-à-vis Day.

PORRAS, FRANCISCO DE (n.d.)
The titular captain of the **caravel** *Santiago* on the **Fourth Voyage,** an incompetent sailor with effective connections with the treasurer of **Castile.** Not only did Porras have to be set aside as captain of the **ship,** but he took a prominent part in a mutiny against CC while the surviving members of the ships' companies were stranded in **Jamaica** in 1504. After the abortive mutiny, CC placed Porras in irons and, when he was rescued in a caravel secured in **Santo Domingo** by **Diego Méndez,** took him and his brother Diego Porras to **Hispaniola** as prisoners. They were set free, however, in Santo Domingo by the governor, **Ovando.**

Ref. *AOS1* II, 316-21, 397-400, 408-17; *AOS2*, II, 585, 650-58.

PORTO SANTO
The smaller of the two inhabited **Madeira** islands, initially settled by Don Bartholomew **Perestrello,** father of CC's wife **Felipa Perestrello e Moniz.** Perestrello was made captain of the island and commissioned to colonize it. He is reputed to have earned the sardonic nickname "Rabbit" when,

in his initial colonizing attempt, he took ashore a pregnant rabbit whose progeny promptly denuded the island of greenery, rendering it a virtual desert for some years. CC and his wife, by some accounts, lived on the island after their marriage around 1497; their son **Diego** may have been born there. At that time the island was in the possession of Felipa's brother, also named Bartholomew Perestrello.

Ref. *AOS*1 I, 40-54; *AOS*2, 38-39.

PORTUGAL

The name of that portion of the western **Iberian Peninsula** along the Atlantic seaboard that remained independent when the rest of the peninsula, united into the Spanish kingdom under **Isabel** of **Castile** and **Ferdinand** of **Aragón,** absorbed **Granada** in 1492. Portugal, hostile to Castile during much of the fifteenth century because of dynastic quarrels and competition for power in the Atlantic, initiated a program of sea exploration in the early part of that century that was aimed at reaching the **Indies** by sailing around Africa. When CC returned from the **First Voyage** in 1492 and visited King **John II** in Portugal before returning to **Spain,** John presumably thought CC had achieved this for the rival Spanish. In 1497, however, the Portuguese navigator **Vasco da Gama** actually did reach India by sailing around Africa.

This initiated a period of Portuguese exploration and conquest that ultimately made the Spanish and Portuguese rivals in the Far East and required that the line of **demarcation** already separating the Spanish and Portuguese areas of influence be extended through the poles to the Eastern Hemisphere. *See* LISBON.

Ref. Edward Gaylord Bourne, "The History and Determination of the Line of Demarcation Established by Pope Alexander VI, between the Spanish and Portuguese Fields of Discovery and Colonization," *Yale Review* 1 (1892): 35-55.

POSTILS

Marginal notes. CC wrote at least 2125 postils in the margins of books he owned, some of which survive in the **Biblioteca Colombina** in **Seville.** The postils frequently contain fascinating information about CC's opinions on a wide variety of subjects, and sometimes provide information about his life, recording, in passing, his experiences in such places as La **Mina** in **Guinea** and the island of **Chios** in the eastern Mediterranean. There is currently considerable discussion over whether CC's postils are largely just the record of his reading during the formation of his **Enterprise of the Indies** in the 1480s, or were written in the middle or late 1490s while he was formulating replies to the critics and enemies who attacked him for various reasons. These books containing CC's postils include a 1477 edition of *Historia Rerum Ubique Gestarum*, a world history written about 1440 by **Aeneas Sylvius;** an edition of about 1480 of **Pierre d'Ailly**'s *Imago Mundi*, a world geography written about 1410; and a 1485 Latin translation of the *Book of Ser Marco Polo.*

Ref. *AOS*1 I, 120-25; *AOS*2, 92-95; Giuseppe Caraci, "A proposito delle 'postille' colombiane," *Pubblicazione dell'Istituto di Scienze Geografiche* (Genoa) 18 (1971): 3-15; Ilaria Luzzana Caraci, "La postilla colombiana B 858 e il suo significato cronologico," *Atti II Convegno Internazionale di Studi Colombiani* (Genoa: CIC, 1977), 197-223; Juan Gil, ed. and trans., *El libro de Marco Polo: version de Rodrigo de Santiella* (Madrid: Alianza, 1987); Louis-André Vigneras, "The Cape Breton Landfall: 1494 or 1497? Note on a letter from John Day," *Canadian Historical Review* 38 (1957): 219-29.

PRESTER JOHN
A legendary medieval Christian prince of the south or east, said, perhaps, to have been the Emperor of Ethiopia. The name frequently occurs in such writings as the *Book of Ser Marco Polo* and the *Travels* of **Sir John Mandeville,** both of which influenced CC's ideas to some degree.

PRIVILEGES, BOOK OF
See **BOOK OF PRIVILEGES.**

PROPHECIES, BOOK OF
See **BOOK OF PROPHECIES.**

PTOLEMY (ca. 100-ca. 170)
Claudius Ptolemaeus, the last great astronomer of classical times, a Graeco-Egyptian geographer and mathematician. He systematized the knowledge of the Alexandrian scientists, including the "Ptolemaic system," a geocentric cosmological theory that goes back at least to Plato. His *Geography* was rediscovered in the early fifteenth century and was highly influential on geographers in CC's time, including **Toscanelli,** emphasizing as it did, the global dominance of the Eurasian land mass stretching from the western ocean to China. King **Ferdinand** purchased a copy in the 1480s, perhaps under the influence of CC's **Enterprise of the Indies.**

PUERTO RICO
The third largest island in the **West Indies,** directly east of **Hispaniola.** CC discovered it on the **Second Voyage** on 19 November 1493 and named it San Juan Batista. The native peoples' name for the island was **Borinquen.**

Ref. *AOS*1 II, 89-90; *AOS*2, 421-22.

Q

The only navigational instrument that CC is known to have employed. This was an arc made of hardwood with sights along one edge through which a heavenly body could be aligned. A plummet line attached to the highest point of the instrument hung alongside a ninety degree scale on the arc to give the altitude of the heavenly body from the horizon. *See* **ASTROLABE.**

Ref. *AOS*1 I, 241-42, 409-10; *AOS*2, 184-85.

QUEEN'S GARDEN
La Jardin de la Reina, an area of small islands in the Caribbean Sea stretching about 140 miles along the southeast coast of **Cuba,** from the Gulf of Guacanayabo to **Trinidad,** extending out from the coast some twenty to fifty miles. CC discovered and explored the area in the spring of 1494 during the **Second Voyage.**

Ref. *AOS*1 II, 129-32; *AOS*2, 454-58.

QUINSAY
A Chinese city, perhaps the one now called Hangchow. According to **Marco Polo,** Quinsay was the capital of a Chinese province named **Mangi.** CC may have thought he was in the province of Mangi when he landed in **Cuba,** and may have thought he was close to the city of Quinsay where he hoped, perhaps, to encounter the great **Khan.**

Ref. *AOS*1 I, 46, 91, 327-38; *AOS*2, 64, 68, 250-51, 256-57.

QUINTERO, CRISTÓBAL (n.d.)
The owner of the *Pinta*, the **ship** commanded by **Martín Alonso Pinzón** on the **First Voyage.** Cristóbal was master of CC's flagship on the **Third Voyage.** His relative, Juan, also a resident of **Palos,** sailed as an able seaman and boatswain on the *Pinta,* and also as master of the *Gallega* on the **Fourth Voyage.**

Ref. *AOS*1 I, 182-91, II, 320; *AOS*2, 118, 140, 147, 160, 585.

QUINTO
Quinto al Mare, a town on the Mediterranean coast a few miles west of **Genoa** where CC's father, Domenico, lived prior to moving to Genoa proper. CC identified himself as being "de terra rubia," (Latin: of red land) and a locale called "terrarossa" (Ital-

ian: redland) was, and still is, part of Quinto.

Ref. Gaetano Ferro, "I luoghi di Columbo e della sua famiglia in Liguria," *La presenza italiana in Andalusia nel basso medioevo. Atti del II Colloquio Italiano-Spagnolo, Roma, 25-27 Maggio 1984* (Bologna: Cappelli, 1986), 135-42; Gianfranco Rovani, *Quinto e Cristoforo Colombo* (Genoa: Edizioni Rovani, 1986).

R

RÁBIDA

A **caravel** on the **Third Voyage.** *See* SHIPS, CC'S.

RÁBIDA, LA
See LA RÁBIDA.

REGIOMONTANUS (1436-1476)

The Latin professional name of a German mathematician, Johannes Müller von Königsberg, teacher of **Martin Behaim** and author of the almanac *Ephemerides.* CC found information in *Ephemerides* about the **lunar eclipse of 1504** which he used to intimidate the Jamaican Indians into giving him support. *See* LUNAR ECLIPSE OF **1504.**

> Ref. *AOS1* I, 99-100, 262-63, II, 400-403; *AOS2*, 76, 653-54; Ernst Zinner, *Leben und Wirken des Johannes Müller von Königsberg genannt Regiomontanus,* 2nd ed. (Munich, 1938; Otto Zeller, Osnabrück, 1968).

RENÉ D'ANJOU (1409-1480)

The monarch of Anjou in southwestern France during CC's youth. In CC's later years, he claimed to have commanded a ship for René, presumably during the hostilities between Anjou and **Aragón.** *See* TUNIS, CC's VOYAGE TO.

> Ref. *AOS1* I, 28-30; *AOS2*, 20-21; R.B. Merriman, *The Rise of the Spanish Empire in the Old World and the New,* vol. 2 (New York: Macmillan, 1936), 56-57.

RESTELO

The town in **Portugal** on the estuary of the **Tagus River** where CC anchored on 4 March 1493 when he returned from the **First Voyage.** CC, invited to visit King **John II,** traveled from Restelo through **Lisbon** and up the Tagus valley to the monastery of **Santa Maria das Virtudes** to see the King before resuming his voyage back to **Palos.**

> Ref. *AOS1* II, 435-44; *AOS2*, 343-47.

RODRIGUEZ DE FONSECA, JUAN (1451-1524)

Archdeacon of **Seville** and later Bishop of Badajoz and chief administrator for the **Indies,** who was in charge of assembling and outfitting CC's fleet for the **Second Voyage.** He seems to have done an excellent job, although he and CC did not like each other and found themselves in a series of conflicts over the business of outfitting the vessels. CC's temperamental and intolerant attitude toward Fonseca is an example of the arrogance that seems to have marked his disposition after his successful return from the **First Voyage.** The conflicts with Fonseca foreshadowed his subsequent disastrous inability to get along with many other Spaniards, including his own colonists, that resulted in his dismissal as **Viceroy of the Indies.**

Ref. *AOS*1 II, 49-55; *AOS*2, 389-90, 394-96, 511, 662.

ROLDÁN, FRANCISCO DE (1462-1502) A Spanish colonist in **Hispaniola** whom CC appointed *alcalde mayor* or chief justice of the island before returning to **Spain** in 1496 at the end of his **Second Voyage.** Roldán, at the center of the growing unrest of the colonists due in part to illness and lack of food and supplies, began a revolt against Columbus while he was away in Spain. When CC returned from Spain on the **Third Voyage,** he and **Bartholomew Columbus** were unable to subdue the rebels entirely and achieved peace only under hu-miliating terms, which included the restoration of Roldán as *alcalde mayor* as well as the institution of a system of **encomiendas,** which gave individual Spanish colonists dominion over a specified plot of land, including the native people already inhabiting that land. CC's failure to command the loyalty of the colonists vis-à-vis Roldán was a strong factor in the **Catholic Monarchs'** decision to send a royal justice, **Francisco de Bobadilla,** to evaluate the situation and take action. Bobadilla decided to arrest CC and his brothers and send them home in chains.

Ref. *AOS*1 II, 295-302; *AOS*2, 563-70; Francisco Domínguez Company, *La Isabela: primera ciudad fundada por Colón en América* (Havana: Sociedad Colombista Panamericana, 1947), Part II, chap. 3 *passim;* Demetrio Ramos Pérez, *El conflicto de las lanzas jinetas: el primo alzamiento en tierra americana, durante el segundo viaje colombino* (Valladolid: Casa-Museo de Colón, 1982). Ramos Pérez's book studies the background of the Roldán revolt.

S

St. Ann's Bay

The bay where CC made **landfall** on the north central coast of **Jamaica** on 5 May 1494 during the voyage of exploration from 24 April to 29 September 1494, starting and ending at **Isabela.** CC named the bay "Santa Gloria" (the Spanish *gloria* means glory, heaven, paradise in English) because of the extreme beauty of the site. On the **Fourth Voyage,** CC ran the two remaining **ships** of his fleet aground at St. Ann's Bay on 25 June 1503 to keep them from sinking and had to remain there stranded with his crew until they were rescued on 29 June 1504 in a ship secured by **Diego Méndez.**

Ref. *AOS*1 II, 123-24, 384-409; *AOS*2, 451-52, 639-58.

St. Brendan's Islands

A legendary group of islands. This archipelago is one of the most persistent myths of medieval folklore. It was supposedly discovered by St. Brendan, the Irish missionary and explorer (sixth century A.D.) and appeared at various points in the Atlantic on countless medieval maps. Three of the islands in the mythical chain were St. Borondon, Lovo, and Capraria.

Ref. *AOS*1 I, 40-41, 80, 215, II, 238; *AOS*2, 28-29, 58, 165, 520.

St. Christopher

CC's patron saint, no longer recognized in the Catholic Church's Liturgical Calendar of Seasons and Feast Days. He was said to be a non-Christian who carried travelers across a river too deep for them to wade as an act of good will and public service. Legend has it that he carried Jesus Christ himself across the water and was appropriately rewarded with sainthood. It is reasonable to believe that CC's name and his tendency to associate himself with the saint were part of the motivation for his lifelong obsession with carrying Christianity across the ocean to non-Christians on the other side.

Ref. *AOS*1 I, 11; *AOS*2, 10.

St. Croix Island

An island at the northwestern end of the **Lesser Antilles,** about 35 miles south of the southernmost of the Virgin Islands, which CC discovered on 13 November 1493 on the **Second Voyage.** Here his landing party had a skirmish with a small but ferocious contingent of **Indians,** perhaps **Caribs,** the first Spanish battle with native Americans.

Ref. *AOS*1 II, 82-85; *AOS*2, 414-18.

St. George, Bank of
See **Bank of St. George.**

St. Vincent, Cape
A promontory at the southwest corner of **Portugal,** known as the Sacred Promontory. The maritime institute of **Henry the Navigator,** responsible for many of the advances in seacraft from which CC was to profit, was located at Sagres, near this promontory. The shipwreck of the Genoese ship *Bechalla* in August 1476, which some historians think left CC stranded in Portugal, took place near Cape St. Vincent.

Ref. *AOS*1 I, 32-41; *AOS*2, 24-29.

Salamanca
The site of the Spanish university of the same name. Some of the hearings of the royal commission appointed by the **Catholic Monarchs** to consider CC's **Enterprise of the Indies** were held at the university. During these meetings CC may have met his long-term friend, the Dominican priest **Diego de Deza** (later Bishop of Palencia and Archbishop of **Seville**), who headed the College of St. Stephen at the university.

Ref. *AOS*1 I, 116-17; *AOS*2, 88-

89; Juan Manzano Manzano, *Cristóbal Colón: siete años decisivos de su vida, 1485-1492* (Madrid: Ediciones Cultura Hispánica, 1964); Henry Vignaud, *Historie Critique de la Grande Entreprise de Christophe Colomb,* vol. 1 (Paris: Welter, 1911), 569-99.

Saltes River
The estuary formed by the confluence of the **Odiel** and **Tinto** Rivers just west of the elevated ground on which the friary of **La Rábida** is built. The Saltes empties into the Mediterranean about two miles southeast of the junction of the Tinto and the Odiel. The fleet of CC's **First Voyage,** embarking from **Palos** about two miles up the Tinto from La Rábida, entered the sea through the Saltes.

Samana Cay
An island in the **Bahamas** southwest of **San Salvador Island.** Samana Cay might be the island of **Guanahani,** the site of CC's **landfall** of 12 October 1492. *See* **Landfall question.**

Ref. G.V. Fox, *An Attempt to Solve the Problem of the First Landing Place of Columbus in the New World* (Washington, DC: Government Printing Office, 1882); Joseph Judge, ''Where Columbus Found the New World,'' *National Geographic* 170 (November 1986): 566-99; John Parker, ''The Columbus Landfall Problem: A Historical Perspective,'' *Terrae Incognitae* 15 (1983): 1-28.

SAN BLAS INDIANS
See CUNA CUNA INDIANS.

SÁNCHEZ DE SEGOVIA, RODRIGO (n.d.)
Royal comptroller (Spanish *veedor real*), whose office was to oversee expenditures on the **First Voyage,** and ensure the Crown's profit share.

Ref. *AOS2*, 146, 224.

SAN JUAN
The *San Juan* and the *Cardera* were the two small **lateen**-rigged **caravels** that CC took, with the square-rigged *Niña*, to explore the coasts of **Cuba** and **Jamaica** in the spring of 1494.

Ref. *AOS1* II, 55-56, 117-18; *AOS2*, 445.

SANLÚCAR DE BARRAMEDA
A town at the mouth of the **Guadal-quivir River** near **Cádiz.** The roadstead at Sanlúcar was a favorite spot for the embarkation and return of expeditions to the **West Indies.** CC's **Third** and **Fourth Voyages** departed from Sanlúcar. It was the site of his last entry into **Spain** at the end of the Fourth Voyage.

Ref. *AOS1* II, 228-33, 322, 410; *AOS2*, 514, 536, 659.

SAN SALVADOR ISLAND
Also called Watlings Island. An island in the **Bahamas** most generally accepted as the actual site of CC's **landfall** of 12 October 1492, although this is disputed. San Salvador Island possesses most of the characteristics of the landfall island (called **Guanahani** by the native inhabitants at that time) that CC described in his *Journal of the First Voyage.* Only one other island, however, is visible from it, and only with difficulty, a fact hard to reconcile with CC's remark that, as he left Guanahani, he could see "so many islands that I could not decide where to go first." The modern San Salvador is not to be confused with CC's San Salvador, the name he gave to Guanahani.

Ref. Joseph Judge, "Where Columbus found the New World," *National Geographic* 170 (November 1986): 566-99; *JOD,* 68; John Parker, "The Columbus Landfall Problem: A Historical Perspective," *Terrae Incognitae* 15 (1983): 1-28.

SANTA CLARA
The **caravel** on the **Third Voyage** nicknamed *Niña*, possibly the same ship as the *Niña* of the **First Voyage.** *See* SHIPS, CC's.

SANTA CRUZ
The **caravel** on the **Third Voyage** nicknamed *India* because it was built in the **West Indies.** *See* SHIPS, CC's.

Ref. *AOS1* II, 173, 176, 180-91, 227-28; *AOS2*, 491, 496-500, 511-12.

SANTA FÉ
A town built by the **Catholic Monarchs** from which they could administer and oversee the siege of the city

of **Granada.** The collapse of Granada and its surrender on 2 January 1492 marked the end of the kingdom of Granada, completing the seven centuries-long effort on the part of the Christian Spanish people to overcome Moorish power on the **Iberian Peninsula.** The **Capitulations of 1492** were signed while the monarchs were still making their capital at Santa Fé. *See* **Moors.**

SANTA FÉ, CAPITULATIONS OF
See CAPITULATIONS OF **1492**

SANTA HERMANDAD
Spanish for "Holy Brotherhood." In medieval times, a name given to confederations of cities that joined to defend themselves from incursions. In 1465 a confederation of the same name was organized in **Castile** to protect travelers from assault, robbery, and kidnapping by the powerful nobles. When **Isabel** came to the throne in 1474, she reorganized this institution as a national police force with jurisdiction over suspects of violent crime captured outside the cities. The Hermandad, supported by taxes on households, accumulated considerable capital, and, in 1492, its co-treasurers **Francisco Pinelli** and **Luis de Santangel** arranged for a loan of 1,140,000 maravedis to the crown to equip the fleet for CC's **First Voyage.**

Ref. C.H. McCarthy, "Columbus and the Santa Hermandad in 1492," *Catholic Historical Review* 1

(1915): 38-50; William Prescott, *History of the Reign of Ferdinand and Isabella,* vol. 1 (London: Rutledge, 1867), 20, 141, 209.

SANTA MARÍA
A square-rigged nao, the flagship of CC's fleet on the **First Voyage.** Somewhat larger and slower than the **caravels** *Pinta* and *Niña,* the *Santa María* set out with a crew of thirty-nine. It was owned by the ship's captain, **Juan de La Cosa.** The *Santa María* ran aground off the north coast of **Haiti** on the evening of 24 December 1492 and was broken up by the surf, but not before CC's crew and natives under the **cacique, Guacanagarí,** had removed the cargo.

The timbers of the wreck were used to construct a makeshift fort named **Navidad,** where CC was forced to leave about forty men as the first European colonists in the **Indies.** All these colonists were massacred by the native peoples before CC returned to Navidad on the **Second Voyage.** There were other ships officially named *Santa María* on CC's subsequent voyages. *See* SHIPS, CC's.

Ref. *AOS1* I, 148-92, 385-95; *AOS2,* 118-29, 139-48, 298-302; Roberto Barreiro Meiro, "Juan de la Cosa y su doble personalidad," *Revista General de Marina* (Madrid) 179 (1970): 165-91; José María Martínez-Hidalgo, *Columbus' Ships,* ed. Howard I. Chapelle

(Barre, MA: Barre Publishers, 1966).

SANTA MARIA DAS VIRTUDES

The monastery where CC visited King **John II** of **Portugal** on 9 March 1493 while his **ship** *Niña* was in **Lisbon** harbor, having taken refuge from an Atlantic **storm** at the end of the eastward crossing of the **First Voyage.**

Ref. *AOS1* I, 438-42; *AOS2*, 343-47.

SANTA MARÍA DE GUÍA

A **caravel** on the **Third Voyage.** *See* SHIPS, CC'S.

SANTA MARÍA DE LA RABIDA

See **LA RABIDA.**

SANTA MARIA ISLAND

The southernmost of the major **Azores Islands** at about thirty-seven degrees North **latitude** and twenty-seven degrees West **longitude.** CC in the *Niña* stopped at this island on the return leg of his **First Voyage** so that his crew could perform votive prayers at a chapel to give thanks for surviving the terrible **storms** the **ship** had encountered. The first contingent of the crew was captured by the captain of the island, **João de Castanheira.** This precipitated a confrontation in which CC succeeded in getting his men back by threatening to send a Spanish contingent to devastate the island.

SANTANGEL, LUIS DE (n.d.)

A financial minister of King **Ferdinand** who, according to CC's son **Ferdinand,** intervened at a crucial juncture in the negotiations between CC and the **Catholic Monarchs** at **Santa Fé** in early 1492, persuading Queen **Isabel** to support the **Enterprise of the Indies** and offering personal financial assistance if needed. As a result of this intervention, the monarchs decided to sponsor the Enterprise. On 4 March 1493, in **Lisbon,** CC dispatched the famous **Letter to Santangel,** intended ultimately for the monarchs, which gave the first written account of the **First Voyage** of discovery.

Ref. *AOS2*, 102-4; Ferdinand Columbus, *The Life of Admiral Christopher Columbus,* ed. and trans., Benjamin Keen (New Brunswick: Rutgers University Press, 1959), chap. 14 *passim.*

SANTANGEL, LETTER TO

See **LETTER TO SANTANGEL.**

SANTIAGO DE PALOS

The **caravel** on the **Fourth Voyage** known to the seamen by the nickname *Bermuda.* Its titular captain was **Francisco de Porras,** who secured the position through connections with the treasurer of **Castile.** The *Bermuda,* infested with worms and sinking, was beached on the north shore of **Jamaica** on 25 June 1503. De Porras led a mutiny against CC while the crew was stranded here.

Ref. *AOS*1 II, 320-43, 366-67. 382-88; *AOS*2, 585, 639-40.

SANTO DOMINGO

The capital of **Hispaniola,** founded by **Bartholomew Columbus** in 1496/ 97 at the mouth of the **Ozama River** on the southeast coast. It replaced the unsatisfactory **Isabela** on the north coast. **Diego Columbus** took his seat at Santo Domingo as second **Viceroy of the Indies** and CC is said to be buried in the cathedral here. Santo Domingo is the modern capital of the Dominican Republic.

SANTO TOMÁS, FORT OF

The first inland European fortress in the **West Indies.** Beginning 12 March 1494, CC conducted an expedition to explore territory south of **Isabela** in **Hispaniola.** After crossing the **Vega Real,** running east and west between the north and the central mountain ranges, CC's expedition climbed the central range and founded the fort to control the central region of this part of the island.

SAONA

An island at the southeastern tip of **Hispaniola,** first sighted by the Savonese **Michele de Cuneo,** who accompanied CC on the voyage from **Isabela** that explored **Cuba** and **Jamaica** in the spring and summer of 1494. CC named the island Saona (Spanish for *Savona*) in honor of

Cuneo, an acquaintance during his youth in **Savona.**

Ref. *AOS*1 II, 158-59.

SÃO TIAGO

An island in the **Cape Verde** archipelago off west Africa where, during the **Third Voyage,** CC stopped to try to get cattle to take to **Hispaniola.** The island was notable for the heavy haze of Sahara desert dust that obscured the mariners' vision.

Ref. *AOS*1 II, 158-59.

SARGASSO SEA

A large, relatively calm oval in the Atlantic, east of the **Bahamas,** south of the Gulf Stream, and north of the main course of the **trade winds,** which is covered with the seaweed sargassum. CC entered the Sargasso Sea at its southern edge on 16 September 1492 during the **First Voyage.** The mariners were concerned about the seaweed until they found it was no impediment to sailing.

Ref. *AOS*1 I, 269-70.

SARMIENTO, CRISTÓBAL GARCÍA (n.d.)

The pilot of the *Pinta* on the **First Voyage.**

Ref. *AOS*1 I, 187.

SAVONA

The port in **Liguria** a few miles west of **Genoa** where CC's father, Domenico, had moved by March 1470. CC, who at this time was about eighteen years old, lived in Savona long enough to have known **Michele de Cuneo,** who accompanied him on the **Second Voyage** and left a colorful account of it.

Ref. *AOS*1 I, 14-15.

SECOND VOYAGE OF DISCOVERY

25 September 1493-11 June 1496. The fleet of seventeen vessels commissioned by the **Catholic Monarchs** to explore, settle, and exploit **Hispaniola** sailed from **Cádiz,** called at the **Canary Islands,** and continued on to the **Lesser Antilles,** entering the archipelago near **Desirade** (or, as CC called it, Deseada) island between **Guadeloupe** and **Dominica,** the avenue of entry that proved best and was routinely used by sailing vessels for centuries thereafter. The **landfall** was on **Mariegalante,** near Dominica, on 3 November 1493.

On Guadeloupe, where the Spaniards encountered native peoples who were probably **Caribs,** an exploring party was lost briefly and an extensive search launched. With the explorers back on board, the fleet sailed northwest along the **Antilles,** discovering **Monserrat, Antigua** (from a distance), Nevis, St. Kitts, **St. Croix,** the Virgin Islands, **Puerto Rico,** and a number of other islands. When the fleet reached its destination, the colony of **Navidad** on the north coast of Hispaniola, CC found the colonists had been massacred to the last man, an ominous event anticipating the continual conflict between Spaniards and native Americans throughout the gradual occupation of the Spanish-American empire.

Unable to sail further east against the **trade winds,** CC founded **Isabela** near the eastern border of what is now **Haiti** and began exploration of **Cuba, Jamaica,** and the south coast of Hispaniola on 24 April 1494, returning on 29 September.

Epidemics and discord made many of the Spanish settlers unhappy, some returning to **Spain** on supply ships, like King **Ferdinand**'s **Fray Bernal Buil,** to spread accounts that damaged CC's reputation. Learning of this, CC returned to defend himself in court. His return fleet, including only the *Niña* and the *India,* brought **Indian slaves** on CC's own initiative to sell to raise revenue for the crown. This further damaged the admiral's relationship with Queen **Isabel,** who did not approve of the enslavement of Spanish subjects. CC arrived in Cádiz on 11 June 1496, concluding the Second Voyage. *See* SHIPS, CC's.

Ref. *EDA*2, 99-139; S.E. Morison, ed. and trans., *The Second Voyage of Christopher Columbus from Cádiz to Hispaniola and the Discovery of the Lesser Antilles* (Oxford: Clarendon, 1939); Kirkpatrick Sale, *The Conquest of Paradise: Christopher Columbus and the Columbian Legacy* (New York: Knopf, 1990), 128-51, 153-66, 208, 381-82*n.*1.

SENECA, LUCIUS ANNAEUS (A.D. 2 or 3-65)

A classical Roman dramatist whose play *Medea* contains a passage that apparently inspired CC, who copied it into his *Book of Prophecies.* Morison's translation reads, "An age will come after many years when the Ocean will lose the chains of things, and a huge land lie revealed; when Tiphys will disclose New Worlds and Thule no longer be the ultimate." CC's son **Ferdinand** wrote, in a note in CC's copy of *Medea,* that his father had fulfilled this prophecy.

Ref. *AOS*1 I, 69, 74, 76.

SEVILLE

Chief city of Andalusia, on the **Guadalquivir River,** said by CC's son **Ferdinand** to be the place where CC first entered **Spain.** During the seven years from 1485 to 1492, while CC was seeking sponsorship of his **Enterprise of the Indies** from the **Catholic Monarchs,** he was frequently in Seville. He appears to have been sponsored in his first audience with the monarchs by **Fray Antonio de Marchena,** a Franciscan astronomer who was the administrator of the Franciscan sub-province of Seville. While he was waiting to learn whether the royal council would report favorably, CC may have worked as a mapmaker and bookseller in Seville. He had contact with the important Genoese families **Spinola** and **di Negro** there and met a number of Flo-rentines, most notably **Francesco Pinelli** and **Amerigo Vespucci,** as well as the Genoese **Juanoto Berardi,** all closely associated with CC's life after the Enterprise of the Indies was approved.

After the discovery of the **New World,** and for centuries afterward, Seville housed the **Casa de Contratación,** the office charged with administration of the conquest and colonization. The papers and records accumulated in this administrative center, known as the **Archive of the Indies,** became the chief archive for historical study of all Spanish activity in the New World. The archive is still housed in the same building constructed for the Casa de Contratación.

SHIPS, CC's

These were mostly **caravels,** but a few were naos or **carracks.** The ships on the **First Voyage** were the caravels *Niña* and *Pinta* and the nao *Santa María.* The seventeen ships of the **Second Voyage** included *Mariagalante,* the flagship, officially named *Santa María; Niña,* officially *Santa Clara,* usually identified with the *Niña* of the first voyage; *San Juan*; *Cardera*; *Gallega*; and *India,* built in **Isabela,** officially *Santa Cruz.* The names of the others on this voyage are not known. On the **Third Voyage** the *Niña* and *India* were sent straight to **Santo Domingo** from **Sanlúcar de Barrameda.** Five others sailed under

CC from **Seville:** *Castilla, Rábida, Gorda, Garza,* and *Santa María de Guía*; these were joined in Sanlúcar by the *Vaqueña.* At the **Canary Islands,** three of these went straight to **Hispaniola** and the others, under CC, sailed a southern route to **Trinidad** and South **America.** The ships on the **Fourth Voyage** were *Capitana,* officially *Santa María; Bermuda,* officially *Santiago de Palos*; Gallega*;* and *Vizcaina.*

Ref. *AOS1* I, xxxv-xli, 149-68 *passim; AOS2,* 113-21 *passim;* Juan Gil, ''El rol del tercer viaje colombino,'' *Historiografía y Bibliografía Americanistas* (Seville) 30 (1985): 83-110; José María Martínez-Hidalgo, ''Las naves de los cuatro viajes de Colón al nuevo mundo,'' *Temi Colombiani* (Genoa: ECIG, 1986), 201-29; Carla Rahn Phillips, ''Sizes and Configurations of Spanish Ships in the Age of Discovery,'' *Proceedings of the First San Salvador Conference: Columbus and His World,* comp. Donald T. Gerace (Ft. Lauderdale: The College Center of the Finger Lakes Bahamian Field Station, 1987), 69-98.

SIERPE, BOCA DE LA

So named by CC. This is the southern and most dangerous egress of the **Gulf of Paría** into which the northern distributaries of the **Orinoco** and the Rio Grande empty. After his discovery of **Trinidad** on the **Third Voyage,** CC sailed through the Boca de la Sierpe, luckily at a time when the current was slack.

Ref. *AOS1* II, 253-59; *AOS2,* 534-40.

SLAVERY AND SLAVE TRADES

The Portuguese slave trade of Africans had been ongoing when CC began his explorations, a practice that was widely condoned at the time, although the **Catholic Monarchs** were ambivalent about the practice. Queen **Isabel**'s policy included the idea that the people residing in Spanish colonies were Spanish subjects. Since Spanish law prohibited the slavery of Spanish subjects, they could not be slaves. Still, CC initiated the enslavement of native Caribbeans, both for trade and for Spanish colonists' use. Since **gold** was not found in promising quantities on the **First Voyage,** CC decided to include **Carib Indians** in the cargo of valuable items he could present to the Sovereigns to trade, and had made plans for a regular trading system. His system of **encomiendas** allowed Spanish colonists to possess any people found on land designated as their property.

Ref. *AOS2,* 32, 291, 486-89, 493, 566, 569; Kirkpatrick Sale, *The Conquest of Paradise: Christopher Columbus and the Columbian Legacy* (New York: Knopf, 1990), 71, 97, 107, 110, 111, 112-13, 122, 123, 126-128, 130-39, 145,

153, 155-56, 166-68, 172, 196, 219-20, 254, 268, 280, 330, 345, 366; Neil L. Whitehead, *Lords of the Tiger Spirit: A History of the Caribs in Colonial Venezuela and Guyana 1498-1820* (Dordrecht/ Providence: Foris Publications, 1988), 9, 22-30, 73-81.

SPAIN

The country occupying all of the **Iberian Peninsula** except the territory of **Portugal.** Spain was politically unified in 1469 with the marriage of **Isabel** of **Castile** and **Ferdinand** of **Aragón.** The two monarchs ruled Castile jointly from 1474 and Aragón jointly from 1479. After Isabel's death in 1504, Ferdinand continued to rule Aragón and Castile as well, as regent for his incompetent daughter Queen Juana. The union became permanent when Juana's son Charles became king of the united Spain in 1516, replacing his mother on the throne.

CC came to Spain with his five-year old son **Diego** in 1485 looking for support for his **Enterprise of the Indies** after the idea was rejected by **John II** of **Portugal.**

SPICE ISLANDS

The **East Indies,** in the sixteenth century called the **Moluccas.**

SPINOLA

A distinguished Genoese family of sea merchants. Along with the **Centurione** and **di Negro** families, the Spinolas figured heavily in the commercial ventures that CC was involved with as a young seaman. It seems likely that CC was among the Ligurians from **Savona** who went to **Chios** in one of the expeditions sponsored by the Spinolas and di Negros in 1475 and 1476. The Spinolas were also among CC's Genoese acquaintances in **Seville,** although it is unlikely that he, as a newcomer without important family credentials, would have associated much with this distinguished family or with any of the other important Genoese in Seville, such as the di Negro and the Centurione families.

Ref. *AOS1* I, 30-31; Giuseppe Pessagno, "Questioni Colombiane," *Atti della Società Liguriana di Storia Patria* (Genoa) 53 (1926): 539-641; Consuelo Varela, "Florentines' Friendship and Kinship with Christopher Columbus," *Proceedings of the First San Salvador Conference: Columbus and His World,* comp. Donald T. Gerace (Ft. Lauderdale: The College Center of the Finger Lakes Bahamian Field Station, 1987), 33-43.

STORMS

In addition to **hurricanes,** CC encountered various storms during the voyages, the worst of which perhaps were those encountered on the return leg of the **First Voyage** from 12 to 15 March 1493. These were not the usual simple circular ocean storms but extremely violent storms marked by well-developed fronts.

Ref. *AOS*1 I, 418-22, 431-34; Charles F. Brooks, "Two Winter Storms Encountered by Columbus in 1493 near the Azores," *Bulletin of the American Meteorological Society* (Milton, MA) 22 (1941): 303-9.

SYLVIUS, AENEAS (1405-1464)

The pseudonym of Enea Silvio Piccolomini, Pope Pius II, author of *Historia Rerum*, a book owned and annotated by CC. *See* POSTILS.

SYPHILIS

The dreaded venereal disease known in Renaissance times as "the great pox," to distinguish it from smallpox; also known variously as the *mal serpentino,* the French disease, the Italian disease, and so on. Many medical scholars who have studied the matter feel that the disease was brought to Europe by the crews or the **Indian** captives on CC's **First Voyage.** The first known European epidemic seems to have begun in **Barcelona,** where CC and his captive Indians were received in state by the **Catholic Monarchs** in 1493. The first medical description of syphilis was made by **Ruy Díaz de Isla,** who mentions among the early sufferers a member of CC's First Voyage named "Pinçón," frequently identified as **Martín Alonso Pinzón,** who was mortally ill when he returned to **Palos** on 15 March 1493.

Ref. *AOS*1 II, 193-218; Francisco Guerra, "The Problem of Syphilis," *First Images of America,* vol. 2, ed. Fredi Chiappelli (Berkeley: University of California Press, 1976), 845-51; M. Lungonelli, "Colombo e il morbo Gallico," *Bolletino del Civico Istituto Colombiano* (Genoa) 1, no. 2 (1953): 51-64.

T

TAGUS RIVER

The river whose estuary forms the port of **Lisbon.** On 4 March 1493, CC took refuge here to escape being wrecked on the rocky shore of **Portugal** on the return leg of his **First Voyage.**

TAINO INDIANS

In CC's time, **Arawak**-speaking people of the **Bahama Islands** and the **Greater Antilles;** the word *Taino* meant "good" or "noble" in their language. Tainos were culturally and linguistically related to the Arawaks of South **America.** They had displaced the Guanahatabey **Indians** to the eastern end of the Greater Antilles about fourteen centuries before CC's **landfall** in 1492, but were being pressed themselves by raids of **Carib Indians** from the **Lesser Antilles.** They may have been the only Indians CC encountered during his **First Voyage.** CC and other Spaniards often erroneously distinguished Tainos from Caribs on the basis of native individuals' cooperation or resistance, respectively.

Ref. *AOS2,* 232-33, 288-90, 294-95, 304, 315, 427, 493, 507, 565; Irving Rouse, "Origin and Development of the Indians Discovered by Columbus," *Proceedings of the First San Salvador Conference: Columbus and His World,* comp. Donald T. Gerace (Ft. Lauderdale: The College Center of the Finger Lakes Bahamian Field Station, 1987), 293-312; Kirkpatrick Sale, *The Conquest of Paradise: Christopher Columbus and the Columbian Legacy* (New York: Knopf, 1990), 65, 97-98, 99-101, 106, 107, 112, 117, 120-21, 122, 130-31, 139, 142, 144, 149, 151, 152-62, 163, 165, 166, 178-79, 200-1, 211, 303.

TALAVERA, FRAY HERNANDO DE (ca. 1428-1507)

A Jeronymite priest, prior of the monastery El Prado near **Valladolid,** confessor of Queen **Isabel,** and subsequent Archbishop of **Granada.** Fray Talavera was a highly respected, frequent agent of the **Catholic Monarchs.** He was appointed head of a royal commission to examine the merits of CC's **Enterprise of the Indies** after CC's royal interview on 26 January 1486. Although the commission did not report favorably on CC's proposal, it is not true that

Talavera felt any antagonism for CC. Talavera, in fact, on 5 May 1492, donated 140,000 maravedis toward CC's **First Voyage.**

Ref. *AOS1* I, 116-19, 131-32; *AOS2*, 88-97; Salvador de Madariaga, *Christopher Columbus: Being the Life of the Very Magnificent Lord Don Cristóbal Colón* (New York: Oxford University Press, 1939), chap. 13 *passim;* Antonio Sánchez Moguel, "Algunos datos nuevos sobre la intervención de Fr. Hernando de Talavera en las negociaciones de Cristóbal Colón con los Reyes Católicos," *Boletin de la Real Sociedad de la Historia* (Madrid) 56 (1910): 154-58.

TEIVE, DIOGO DE (n.d.)

A Portuguese navigator who, in 1452, discovered the far-western **Azores** islands of **Flores** and **Corvo,** the second of which was only a little more than a thousand miles from **Newfoundland.** Teive's pilot on this voyage was Pedro Vásquez de la Frontera, who was living in **Palos** in 1492, and who told CC and **Martín Alonso Pinzón** that he had information about the **Indies** and encouraged the mariners to make the voyage they were planning. Vasquez may have been the same pilot Pedro de Velásquez, native of the **Huelva** area, who had returned home after long service as a pilot for **Portugal.**

Ref. *AOS1* I, 41, 80, 182-83; *AOS2*, 29, 58, 140-41; Jaime Cortesão, "El viaje de Diogo de Teive," *El viaje di Diogo de Teive. Colón y los Portugueses* (Valladolid: Casa-Museo de Colón, 1975), 9-29; Antonio Rumeu de Armas, *La Rábida y el descubrimiento de América: Colón, Marchena, y fray Juan Pérez* (Madrid: Cultura Hispánica, 1968), chap. 4 *passim.*

TENERIFE ISLAND

One of the largest of the **Canary Islands,** located between **Grand Canary** and **Gomera.** It is distinguished by its snowcapped, occasionally active volcano. Because the native peoples were powerfully hostile toward being overrun by the invaders, Tenerife was not occupied by the Spanish in 1492 and was only conquered a few years later by Alonso de Lugo, who married **Beatriz de Bobadilla y Peraza,** ruler of Gomera and the reputed romantic interest of CC. The marriage came after CC's second visit to her island in 1493, on his **Second Voyage.**

TERREROS, PEDRO DE (d. 1504)

CC's personal steward on the **Second Voyage** and commander of the **ship** *Gallega* on the **Fourth Voyage.**

Ref. *AOS1* I, 188, 191, II, 229-64 *passim,* 320-27, 414; *AOS2*, 396, 445, 543, 585, 589, 663.

TERRESTRIAL PARADISE

Term used by medieval scholars to describe the biblical Garden of Eden, the place where life was created. According to a tradition honored by Dante, Eden was near the top of a high mountain at the ultimate point of the East, a point where the earth's surface rose in the form of a pear or a woman's breast, with the stem or nipple somewhere near the equator.

On the **Third Voyage,** when CC landed in **Venezuela** at the mouth of the **Orinoco,** he thought he had reached the Terrestrial Paradise. His medieval authority on world history, **Pierre d'Ailly,** would have put him in touch with this traditional myth.

> Ref. *AOS*1 II, 282-85; *AOS*2, 556-58; Dante Alighieri, *Purgatorio*, Cantos 30-33; Leonard Olschki, "Ponce de León's Fountain of Youth: the History of a Geographical Myth," *Hispanic American Historical Review* 21 (1941): 361-85.

THIRD VOYAGE OF DISCOVERY

30 May 1498-October 1500. CC set out from **Sanlúcar de Barrameda,** at the mouth of the **Guadalquivir River,** with six **ships,** stopping for supplies at **Porto Santo, Madeira,** and **Gomera** before reaching **Ferro,** where he split the fleet. *Rábida, Garza* and an unnamed ship, carrying supplies for **Hispaniola,** were sent directly to **Santo Domingo.** CC took the remaining three-ship exploration fleet, *Santa María de Guía, Castilla,* and *Gorda,* to the **Cape Verde Islands,** then south of his previous Atlantic routes, achieving **landfall** at **Trinidad** on 31 July 1498. CC discovered South **America** at that mouth of the **Orinoco** that empties into the **Gulf of Paría** and, apparently overlooking the fabulously wealthy oyster beds of the **Pearl Coast,** sailed for Hispaniola, making landfall at **Beata Island** on 20 August 1498. Near this point he encountered his brother **Bartholomew,** who had seen the first part of CC's fleet sail west, past Santo Domingo harbor, and had sailed out to intercept and redirect them. The brothers decided to return to Santo Domingo and reached it, against the **trade winds,** on 31 August.

The next two years witnessed the gradual collapse of CC's administration as the Spanish colonists became increasingly dissatisfied with the situation, and a revolt under **Roldán** developed. When the **Catholic Monarchs** perceived that CC was unable to arrest the progressive deterioration they sent a justice, **Francisco de Bobadilla,** to put things in order. Arriving in Santo Domingo on 23 August 1500, he quickly decided to send CC and his brothers home in irons. CC, aboard the caravel *Gorda,* refused the captain's offer to remove the bonds, and wore them until he was received by the sovereigns in

December, after docking at **Cádiz** in late October.

Ref. *AOS*1 II, 232-93; *AOS*2, 515-61; Juan Gil, "El rol del tercer viaje colombino," *Historiografía y Bibliografía Americanistas* (Seville) 30 (1985): 83-110; J.H. Parry, *The Discovery of South America* (London: Elek, 1979); Kirkpatrick Sale, *The Conquest of Paradise: Christopher Columbus and the Columbian Legacy* (New York: Knopf, 1990), 58, 129, 169, 170-83; L.A. Vigneras, *The Discovery of South America and the Andalusian Voyages* (Chicago: University of Chicago Press, 1976).

TINTO

A river of southwestern **Spain** that joins the **Odiel River** near the Portuguese frontier to form the **Saltes,** which then empties into the Atlantic Ocean several miles from the junction. The town of **Palos,** the embarkation and **landfall** point of the **First Voyage** and supplier of two **ships,** the *Niña* and *Pinta*, lies on the Tinto River. Also, the friary of **La Rábida,** where CC found critical support for his **Enterprise of the Indies,** is located on the Tinto. CC's son **Diego** may have been educated at La Rábida.

Ref. *AOS*1 I, 107-19 *passim; AOS*2, 79-80.

TÍTULO OF 1492

The royal confirmation of CC's titles and offices as promised in the **Capitulations of 1492,** contingent on his discovery and acquisition for **Spain** of island(s) or mainland as a result of the voyage.

Ref. *AOS*1 I, 139-40; *AOS*2, 105.

TOBACCO

The Europeans first saw tobacco being smoked in **Cuba** during the expedition led by **Luis de Torres** on the **First Voyage,** which explored inland from the northeast coast from 1 to 5 November 1492. The Spaniards had probably seen tobacco on 16 October in the possession of an **Indian** they found in a **canoe** in the **Bahamas,** but he was not smoking at the time.

Ref. *AOS*1 I, 317, 342; *AOS*2, 261.

TOLEDO, ARCHBISHOP OF
See MENDOZA.

TOLEDO, MARIA DE COLÓN Y
See COLÓN Y TOLEDO.

TORDESILLAS, TREATY OF
See PAPAL BULLS.

TORRES, ANTONIO DE (d. 1502)
The brother of **Doña Juana de Torres,** governess of the **Catholic Monarchs'** son **Prince Don Juan.** He owned the *Mariagalante,* the flagship on the outward leg of CC's **Second Voyage** and commanded the fleet when CC sent twelve of the seventeen vessels back to **Spain** after landing the colonists in early 1494. Torres also com-

manded a fleet of four supply ships that brought provisions to CC and his colonists in **Isabela** in the fall of 1494. Torres and his supply fleet departed in February 1495 to return to Spain carrying, among others, the acquaintance of CC's youth from **Savona, Michele de Cuneo** and the Indian **Diego Colón,** whom CC sent home to counter **Fray Bernal Buil** and other malcontents who had returned with Torres in early 1494, spreading damaging reports about CC. Torres died in the **hurricane** that struck the bullion fleet that left **Santo Domingo** in the early summer of 1502. The **ship** he commanded went down with all hands, including CC's enemy **Francisco de Bobadilla** and the Indian **cacique Guarionex.**

Ref. *AOS1* II, 105-6, 167-70, 210-11; *AOS2,* 435, 485-86, 590.

TORRES, BARTOLOMÉ DE (n.d.)
A member of CC's crew on the **First** and **Second Voyages.** When CC was recruiting his crew in the summer of 1492, Torres was in jail in **Palos** awaiting execution for killing a man in a fight. He was released by three of his friends: Alonso Clavijo, Juan de Moguer, and Pedro Yzquierdo and the four together enlisted and served in the crew of CC's flagship *Santa María.* Torre's liberators were sentenced to death *in absencia* but all were pardoned by the crown on their return in 1493 for their service. These circumstances led to stories that CC employed convicts for his First Voyage.

Ref. *AOS1* I, 184, 192; Alicia Bache Gould, "Nuevos datos sobre Colón y otros descubridores: Datos nuevos sobre el primer viaje de Colón," *Boletin de la Real Academia de la Historia* (Madrid) 76 (1920): 201-14.

TORRES, JUANA DE (n.d.)
The sister of **Antonio de Torres** and governess of the monarchs' son **Prince Don Juan,** with whom CC's sons, **Diego** and **Ferdinand Columbus,** were schooled. At the end of the **Third Voyage** CC, who was on good terms with her, wrote her a letter that expressed his outrage at being judged harshly for his methods in attempting to bring peace to **Santo Domingo,** a frontier colony. This was the voyage from which CC returned in chains, sent home for judgement by **Francisco de Bobadilla.**

Ref. *AOS1* II, 304, 309; *AOS2,* 572; *JOD,* 289-98, text of the letter.

TORRES, LUIS DE (n.d.)
A **converso,** or **Jew** who converted to Christianity, whom CC took along as interpreter on the **First Voyage.** Since he knew various languages, including some Hebrew and Arabic, it was thought that he might be able to converse with the Asians the fleet might encounter.

Ref. *AOS*1 I, 187, 341-42; *AOS*2, 145, 257-58, 261, 306.

TOSCANELLI, PAOLO DEL POZZO (1397-1482)
The Florentine physician and cosmographer who, in 1474, wrote to **Fernão Martins,** a representative in Rome of King **John II** of **Portugal,** urging the king to sponsor a voyage of exploration westward to discover a new route to the **East Indies.** CC corresponded with Toscanelli and he sent CC a copy of the letter he had written to Martins. It is unlikely that CC got his original idea for the **Enterprise of the Indies** from this letter, but he was very much encouraged by Toscanelli's opinion that Asia was within reasonable sailing distance of Portugal.

Ref. *AOS*1 I, 45-47, 56-58, 85-86; *AOS*2, 33-34, 63-65, 78; Thomas Goldstein, *Dawn of Modern Science* (Boston: Houghton Mifflin, 1980), 15-29; Charles E. Nowell, "The Toscanelli Letters and Columbus," *Hispanic American Historical Review* 17 (1937): 346-48.

TRADE WINDS
The steady prevailing winds blowing east to west in bands extending several hundred miles south from about the tropic of Cancer and north from about the tropic of Capricorn in both the Atlantic and the Pacific Oceans. One of CC's most important achievements was to recognize that sailing west in the trade wind **latitudes** was the key to a rapid crossing.

TREATIES
See **PAPAL BULLS.**

TREVISAN, ANGELO DE (n.d.)
Also known as Angelo Trivigiano, a Venetian who, in *Libretto de tutta la navigatione* (1504), describes CC as "a tall man, well built, ruddy, of great creative talent, and with a long face." Trevisan translated this manuscript, thought to have been composed ca. 1501 by **Peter Martyr,** into Venetian in 1504. It is the earliest known published account of CC's first three voyages. In about 1507 Trevisan compiled a narrative account of a reputed voyage from **Hispaniola** to the **Pearl Coast** which has sometimes been included in some accounts of CC's **Second** or **Third Voyage;** but CC scholars are generally very skeptical about the likelihood that CC ever made or sponsored such a voyage.

Ref. *AOS*1 I, 8, II, 289-90; *AOS*2, 43; Charles E. Nowell, "Reservations Regarding the Historicity of the 1494 Discovery of South America," *Hispanic American Historical Review* 22 (1942): 205-10; W.J. Wilson, "The Historicity of the 1494 Discovery of South America," *Hispanic American Historical Review* 22 (1942): 193-205; W.J. Wilson, "The Spanish Discovery of the South American

Mainland,'' *Geographical Review* 31 (1941): 283-99.

TRIANA, RODRIGO DE (d. ca. 1525)

The seaman aboard the *Pinta* who first reported seeing land at the time of CC's **landfall** at **Guanahani** or **San Salvador Island** in the **Bahamas**, at 2 A.M., 12 October 1492. CC claimed to have seen a light on the land at about 10 P.M., 11 October, and successfully claimed the 10,000 maravedi annual pension promised by the monarchs to the person who first sighted land. Triana became a master mariner in 1507 and was chief pilot in 1525 on Losoya's **Moluccas** expedition, in which he perished.

Ref. *AOS1* I, 298, 311; *AOS2*, 226; Angel Ortega, *La Rábida: historia documental crítica,* vol. 2 (Seville: Editorial de San Antonio, 1925-26), 218-21.

TRINIDAD

An island off the coast of **Venezuela,** west of the chief mouth of the **Orinoco River** where it empties into the **Gulf of Paría.** CC discovered Trinidad when he made his **landfall** on 31 July 1498 after crossing the Atlantic on his **Third Voyage.**

Ref. *AOS1* II, 246-47, 253-56; *AOS2*, 528-40.

TRISTAN, DIEGO (d. 1503)

A gentleman volunteer in CC's crew on the **Fourth Voyage** who advanced to become captain of the *Capitana.* He was killed on 6 April 1503 in the battle between the crew and the **Indians** at CC's settlement of Santa María de Belén at the mouth of the **Belén** River in **Panama.**

Ref. *AOS2*, 396, 445, 584, 629.

TUNIS, CC'S VOYAGE TO

In **Ferdinand Columbus**'s biography of his father, the *Historie*, CC claims to have sailed as captain of a ship for King **René d'Anjou,** presumably in the early 1470s, and to have deceived his seamen about the compass in order to sail across the Mediterranean to Tunis to capture a ship for the king. The voyage, as Ferdinand has CC describe it, is so rapid (Sardinia to Tunis overnight), and the compass trick so bizarre, that scholars have doubted that it ever occurred in the way it is reported.

Ref. *AOS1* I, 28; Ferdinand Columbus, *The Life of the Admiral Christopher Columbus,* ed. and trans. Benjamin Keen (New Brunswick: Rutgers University Press, 1959), chap. 4 *passim.*

TURKS AND CAICOS ISLANDS

A group of islands at the south end of the **Bahamas** chain. Both **Grand Turk Island,** the most westerly of the group, and the several Caicos islands have sometimes been designated as **Guanahani,** site of CC's **landfall** of the **First Voyage.** Grand Turk is persistently named for the honor, since it closely matches CC's description of the island, which he called **San Salvador,** in his *Journal.* Moreover, unlike San Salvador Island or **Samana Cay,** there are many islands visible from it, corresponding closely with CC's remark in the *Journal* that, leaving San Salvador, he could see "so many islands that I could not decide where to go first."

Ref. *JOD,* 68; R.H. Power, "The Discovery of Columbus' Island Passage to Cuba, 12-27 October 1492," *Terrae Incognitae* 15 (1983): 151-72; Pieter Verhoog, "Columbus Landed on Caicos," *Terrae Incognitae* 15 (1983): 29-34.

V

VALLADOLID

A city in Old **Castile,** site of a major university, where King **Ferdinand** had his main seat during CC's last years, from 1505 to 1506. CC went to Valladolid in 1505 shortly after he returned from the **Fourth Voyage** and spent a great deal of time trying to press his claims for the privileges granted him in the **Capitulations of 1492.** CC bought or rented a house for himself and died there on 20 May 1506; no one knows which house it was. His body was initially buried in the Church of San Francisco, but in 1509 was moved to **Seville** and then to **Santo Domingo,** following the wishes of **Diego Columbus,** his son.

Ref. *AOS1* II, 418-23; *AOS2,* 667-69; V.M. Fernández de Castro, "Lo que hay sobre la Casa de Colón en Valladolid," *Revista Literaria* (Valladolid) 10 April 1878; R. Vázquez Illa, "La Casa de Colón en Valladolid," *Boletin de la Sociedad Geografía de Madrid* 24 (1888): 22-31.

VAQUEÑA

A ship on the **Third Voyage.** *See* **SHIPS, CC'S.**

VÁSQUEZ, PEDRO DE LA FRONTERA

See **TEIVE, DIOGO DE.**

VEGA REAL

A fertile agricultural valley in **Hispaniola,** south of CC's initial settlement of **Isabela,** extending northwest to southeast between the coastal and central mountain ranges. CC's first **gold**-seeking expedition into the interior of the island, which began on 12 March 1494, proceeded south from Isabela over the coastal range through the pass named "Puerto de los Hidalgos." It continued due south into the valley, following a trail that crossed the river Yaque del Norte at Ponton, and to the site in the central mountains near to what is now the village of Janico, where CC was to construct his fort, **Santo Tomás.**

On 27 March 1495, during the **Second Voyage,** CC led a force of Spaniards that defeated the native peoples under **Guatiguana** in the Vega Real.

Ref. *AOS1* II, 109-13, 170-71; *AOS2,* 438-42, 488-89.

VENEZUELA

A South American country on the

south coast of the Caribbean Sea, discovered by CC on 1 August 1498 on the **Third Voyage,** when he sighted land to the south from a place just west of Erin Point on the south coast of **Trinidad.** The place he sighted was probably Punta Bombeador on the **Orinoco** delta. He entered the **Gulf of Paría** through the **Boca de la Sierpe** west of Erin Point, recognizing that the fresh water in the gulf was the effluence of a large river which could only come from a continent; however, he might not have recognized at the time that this continent was distinct from the far eastern mainlands he was seeking, even though he described what he had found as *"otro mundo,"* another world. He explored the Gulf of Paría and saw pearls on the native peoples he found there. He departed through one of the **Boca del Dragon** but did not pause to explore the nearby Margarita Island just off the Venezuelan coast. Consequently, CC missed finding the rich pearl fishery there, later discovered by **Alonso de Hojeda** and exploited by **Peralonso Niño.** *See* TERRESTRIAL PARADISE.

Ref. *AOS*1 II, 254, 259-81, 290, 300; *AOS*2, 533, 536-55, 568.

VERAGUA

The region in the territory of **Panama** that CC sailed along and explored from 17 October to 31 December 1502, during the **Fourth Voyage,** seeking a strait to the Indian Ocean. In 1536, when the widow of **Diego Columbus, Doña María de Colón y Toledo,** renounced the hereditary titles and privileges of the admiral on behalf of her son **Luis Colón,** Luis was given twenty-five square leagues in the territory of Veragua in compensation and the title Duke of Veragua, a title that the family has retained ever since.

Ref. *AOS*1 II, 350-53, 366-76; *AOS*2, 609-33.

VESPUCCI, AMERIGO (1451-1512)

The Florentine who made a reputation for himself as a navigator, exploring the **Venezuelan** coast with **Hojeda** in 1499 and, in 1501/02, under the sponsorship of the King of **Portugal,** the western coast of South **America** to the Brazilian bulge. CC and Vespucci were friends. The first evidence of the relationship is in Vespucci's dealings with CC's business partner, **Juanoto Berardi,** from 1493 to 1495. Apparently the good relations were never broken, CC writing to **Diego** on 5 February 1504 of his affection for Vespucci.

Vespucci's *Lettera* to Soderini contains an account of Vespucci's voyage to the **New World** in 1497; this, in conjunction with his *Mundus Novus,* apparently gained a reputation of authenticity by predating **Angelo Trevisan**'s translation of *Libretto de tutta la navigatione* in 1504, a manuscript that contains an account of CC's first three voyages. The timing of the *Lettera* led to an historical controversy over whether Vespucci intended to usurp CC's fame. The controversy was fed by the fact that Vespucci had managed to give his name to the New World lands—America. However, **Martin Waldseemüller,** a cosmographer in service to the Duke of Lorraine (who had received a copy of Vespucci's letter to Soderini) seems to have been responsible for circulating the feminine variation of Vespucci's first name as the name of the New World. As an appendix to his *Cosmographiae Introductio* (1507), he printed a Latin translation of Vespucci's letter along with a justification for the name "America"; his map of 1507 also carried the name to designate what is now South America. *See* **Letter to Santangel.**

Ref. *AOS*1 II, 416-17; Roberto Almagià, "A proposito dei viaggi di Amerigo Vespucci," *Revista Geografica* (Florence) 42 (1935): 49-56; Ilaria Luzzana Caraci, *Colombo e Amerigo Vespucci* (Genoa: Edizioni Culturali Internazionali Genova, 1987).

Viceroy of the Indies
A title accorded to CC as one of the privileges of the **Capitulations of 1492,** making him the surrogate for the Spanish monarchs. While not formally removed during his lifetime, the **Catholic Monarchs** ceased to honor this title when they replaced CC as governor of **Hispaniola** with **Ovando.** The title was inherited by **Diego Columbus** and **Luis Colón,** though not much recognized by the crown after about 1512.

Virtudes
See **Santa Maria das Virtudes.**

Vizcaina
One of CC's four **caravels** on the **Fourth Voyage,** commanded by **Bartolomeo Fieschi,** a Genoese acquaintance of CC, and owned by Juan Pérez (not the priest of the same name), who sold the **ship** to CC during the voyage. The ship had to be abandoned at Porto Bello, **Panama,** having been eaten full of holes by shipworms during the long, rainy exploration.

Ref. *AOS*1 II, 321, 329 *n.* 4, 327-79 *passim; AOS*2, 585, 592, 634.

Vizinho, José (n.d.)
A Jewish physician, mathematician, and cosmologist at the court of **John II** of **Portugal** who translated the *Ephemerides* of **Zacuto** and was an expert in determining **latitude.**

Ref. *AOS*2, 69-70, 527.

Voyages of Discovery
See individual entries for **First Voyage, Second Voyage, Third Voyage, Fourth Voyage.**

W

WALDSEEMÜLLER, MARTIN (ca. 1470-1522)

The German geographer whose map bearing the name "**America**" appears in the *Cosmographiae Introductio* published in St. Dié on 25 April 1507, establishing the name as a label for the **New World.** *See* **AMERIGO VESPUCCI.**

WATLINGS ISLAND
See **SAN SALVADOR ISLAND.**

WEST INDIES

An archipelago in the Caribbean Sea extending from just south of the Florida Keys to just north of the island of **Trinidad.** The islands are arranged roughly in the shape of a rake, with the horizontal handle consisting of the **Greater Antilles** (including **Cuba, Jamaica, Hispaniola,** and **Puerto Rico**) and the vertical head consisting of the **Lesser Antilles.**

When CC discovered Cuba and Hispaniola on his **First Voyage,** he assumed that he had found the **Indies** of the Indian Ocean, which were known to be a major source of spices; until the **Magellan** voyage the two archipelagos were identical in the Spanish mind. The discovery that the archipelagos are different led to the labeling of the Caribbean Indies as "West" and the other archipelago as "East." *See* **EAST INDIES.**

WINDWARD PASSAGE

The strait between **Hispaniola** to the east and **Cuba** and **Jamaica** to the west, so named because it is situated windward of Cuba when the **trade winds** are blowing. One of the great feats of the **Fourth Voyage** was **Diego Méndez's** successful upwind **canoe** crossing of this strait from Jamaica to Hispaniola to get aid for CC and his stranded crew.

Ref. *AOS1* I, 362-63, II, 394-96; *AOS2*, 277-78, 647-49.

X

XARAGUA

The peninsula that extends westward toward **Cuba** on the southwest corner of **Hispaniola,** where the chieftaincy of the native **cacique Behechio,** and later, **Anacoana,** was located. The rebels led by **Roldán** based their activities in Xaragua.

Ref. *AOS*1 II, 295-97; *AOS*2, 563-64.

Z

ZACUTO, ABRAHAM (ca. 1450-ca. 1520)

A Jewish rabbi and professor of mathematics at **Salamanca** who prepared an *Ephemerides,* or nautical calendar, translated for **John II** of **Portugal** by Zacuto's pupil **José Vizinho.**

Ref. *AOS*1 I, 92-93; *AOS*2, 69-70, 185.